# ACTION RESEARCH ON BLOCK SCHEDULING

## David Marshak

EYE ON EDUCATION
6 DEPOT WAY WEST, SUITE 106
LARCHMONT, NY 10538
(914) 833–0551
(914) 833–0761 fax

ISBN 1-883001-40-4

**Library of Congress Cataloging-in-Publication Data**

Marshak, David.
    Action research on block scheduling / by David Marshak.
        p.      cm.
    ISBN   1-883001-40-4
    1. Schedules, School—United States—Case studies. 2. Action research in education—United States—Case studies. 3. High Schools—United States—Case studies. I. Title.
LB3032.M35    1997                       97-10138
371.2'42—dc21
                                             CIP

10 9 8 7 6 5 4 3 2 1

Editorial and production services provided by Richard H. Adin Freelance Editorial Services, 9 Orchard Drive, Gardiner, NY 12525 (914-883-5884)

## Also Published by Eye On Education:

**Teaching in the Block:**
**Strategies for Engaging Active Learners**
Edited By Robert Lynn Canady and Michael D. Rettig

**Block Scheduling: A Catalyst for Change in High Schools**
By Robert Lynn Canady and Michael D. Rettig

**The Performance Assessment Handbook**
**Vol. 1. Portfolios and Socratic Seminars**
By Bil Johnson

**The Performance Assessment Handbook**
**Vol. 2. Performances and Exhibitions**
By Bil Johnson

**The School Portfolio:**
**A Comprehensive Framework for School Improvement**
By Victoria Bernhardt

**Instruction and the Learning Environment**
By James Keefe and John Jenkins

**Research on Educational Innovations, 2d ed.**
By Arthur Ellis and Jeffrey Fouts

**Research on School Restructuring**
By Arthur Ellis and Jeffrey Fouts

**Educational Technology:**
**Best Practices from America's Schools**
By William Bozeman and Donna Baumbach

**Hands-on Leadership Tools for Principals**
By Ray Calabrese, Gary Short, and Sally Zepeda

**The Reflective Supervisor: A Practical Guide for Educators**
By Ray Calabrese and Sally Zepeda

**Handbook of Educational Terms and Applications**
By Arthur Ellis and Jeffrey Fouts

**Leadership and Collaboration: Alternatives to the Hierarchy**
By Michael Koehler and Jeanne Baxter

**The Principal as Steward**
By Jack McCall

**The Principal's Edge**
By Jack McCall

**Directory of Innovations in Elementary Schools**
By Jane McCarthy and Suzanne Still

**School-to-Work**
By Arnold Packer and Marion Pines

**The Educator's Brief Guide to Computers in the Schools**
By Eugene F. Provenzo, Jr.

**Innovations in Parent and Family Involvement**
By J. William Rioux and Nancy Berla

# ACKNOWLEDGMENTS

Many thanks to all of the Washington State teachers who participated in this project, including those whose work appears in this volume and our other project colleagues who contributed to our work together. I appreciate and admire their professionalism, curiosity, and commitment to learning and teaching.

Special thanks to Dr. MAK Mitchell, superintendent, and Dr. Linda Averill, assistant superintendent, of the Shoreline, Washington School District for their sponsorship of the project, and to Dorothy Johnson of the Shoreline School District for her administration of the project.

I am grateful to Bob Sickles for his belief in the value of our work and his commitment to its publication.

# ABOUT THE AUTHOR

*David Marshak,* currently assistant professor at Seattle University, taught in public high schools and alternative high schools in Connecticut and New Hampshire. He received his doctorate in teaching, curriculum, and learning environments from Harvard University Graduate School of Education. He also served as Curriculum and Assessment Coordinator for Addison Northeast school district in Vermont, and is Senior Editor of the hm Learning and Study Skills Programs, published by the National Association of Secondary School Principals.

# TABLE OF CONTENTS

# INTRODUCTION

## THE CONVENTIONAL STRUCTURES OF HIGH SCHOOL

The conventional structures of the American high school, which continue to dominate the educational landscape in this last decade of the twentieth century, are nearly 100 years old. In 1892, the *Report of the Committee of Ten* codified the subject core of the curriculum—English, mathematics, science, history, geography, modern languages—and its departmental organization. Each subject would be taught separately by a different teacher. The creation of regional accreditation organizations and the implementation of accreditation procedures around the turn of the century further entrenched these curricular and departmental structures.

In 1906, the Carnegie Foundation for the Advancement of Teaching established what came to be known as the Carnegie unit: 120 clock hours of class time devoted to a subject. Within a few years, the model of 45-minute periods for 180 days, totaling 120 hours and one Carnegie unit, became the scheduling norm in high schools. With 45-minute periods came the six-, seven-, or eight-period day. Within this norm, just as materials moved along an assembly line to be fashioned into finished products, students moved from teacher to teacher to be filled with knowledge efficiently and harmoniously.

In 1918, the National Educational Association's *Report on the Reorganization of Secondary Education* solidified the normative status of the comprehensive high school with separate college preparation and general education tracks. Because the report envisioned the comprehensive high school as a modern day "common school," both tracks would focus on a similar curriculum, with students in the general track receiving a less challenging version of the college preparatory studies.

Two additional elements contributed to the definition of the conventional structures. The first focused on the belief held by most policymakers and educators that learning took place through the transmission of information from teacher to student. Disagreeing with John Dewey's notions of the importance of meaning in the learning process, the common wisdom maintained that students were in fact "empty vessels" whose minds needed to be filled with knowledge. Teaching was primarily an activity of distributing information, and learning was primarily an activity of receiving it. Informed by this understanding, lecture became the primary teaching method in high schools. Teachers talked and students listened. Within the conventional high school today, even though teachers use many other kinds of activities within 45–50-minute periods, lecture is dominant. Teachers present material, and students are supposed to receive it. Teachers cover the topics in the curriculum and, to a great extent, the measure of instruction is coverage of the curriculum, not student learning.

The second additional element in the conventional structures is that when teachers lectured, they did so alone. Each teacher taught his or her 30 students alone. Perhaps once or twice a year the principal would enter the classroom for a brief evaluation visit. But other than that, teaching was a solitary activity conducted without interaction with other adults.

These are the central elements of the conventional high school in the United States, a set of structures based partly on nineteenth century categories of knowledge and models of learning, and partly on early twentieth century ideas of industrial efficiency. This model of high school is still normative, still dominant in high schools today.

The additional element of larger and increasingly bureaucratic and impersonal schools, already common in large cities, entered into high school norms nationwide. This came about as a result of James Bryant Conant's report, *The American High School Today*, and his subsequent campaign for larger high schools. By 1970, nearly two-thirds of high school students were enrolled in schools with graduating classes of 200 students or more.

Prior to the present decade, this conventional model of high school received two significant challenges. In the decades of its origins, John Dewey and an array of "progressive" educators challenged its lack of connection both to young people's immediate experience of life and to adult life outside of school, as well as its segregation of studies based on narrowly drawn subject areas. In the "culture war" of the first quarter of this century, the industrial model of organization, which was transforming the economic and social life of American society, easily defeated Dewey and his allies in the struggle for the definition of high school.

A second challenge arose in the late 1960s. In what turned out to be a brief window of opposition, perhaps from 1967 to 1974, critics of the conventional high school attacked its lack of humaneness and relevance as well as its racism, essentially a restatement of Dewey's critique with a new strand of criticism drawn from the civil rights revolution of the 1960s. Yet, despite the commotion of the attack on the conventional structures—in best-selling books and mass circulation magazines, and in the then relatively new medium of television—and despite the creation of thousands of free schools and alternative schools, albeit mostly short-lived, throughout the nation, the period of challenge was brief. By 1974, the conventional structures, never really threatened in practice, were no longer a focus of criticism as politicians and educators turned their attention "back to basics."

In 1971, the Association for Supervision and Curriculum Development's Council on Secondary Education published *Removing Barriers to Humaneness in the High School*. The editors J. Gaylen Saylor and Joshua L. Smith entitled their introduction, which encapsulated a good portion of the critique of the conventional high school, "We Can Escape From the Box." Wishful thinking: A quarter century later, history shows that the box—the conventional structures—emerged from that period strengthened: larger high schools, a rejection of team teaching and integrated subjects, increased tracking of students, a reaffirmation of the "basic subjects" as defined by the Committee of Ten and of the Carnegie unit, and a continuation of 45–50-minute period. This is the history to date.

# BLOCK PERIODS:
# STEPS TOWARD A NEW MODEL OF HIGH SCHOOL?

In the last 5 years, a new challenge to the conventional high school has arisen in the form of block-period schedules. This is a new effort to escape from "the box" and to create structures for high school based on some very different understandings of human development, learning and teaching, the nature and structure of knowledge, and the cultural and social realities of the present, as well as expectations for the future, than were commonly held either in 1920 or in 1970.

By the fall of 1995, a considerable momentum had grown both in Washington State and in other regions of the United States for dramatically increasing the length of class periods in high schools. In place of the 45–55-minute, six- to eight-period day, which had been the norm for nearly a century, a critical number of high schools were experimenting with periods nearly twice as long—80–100 minutes—or even longer, with only 3 or 4 periods each day.

One striking aspect of this wave of innovation and experimentation was the lack of literature and resources available to high school teachers who had chosen to teach in this longer time frame about what constituted effective teaching and learning practice in block periods. There were some sources available pertaining to the scheduling of block-period days, particularly relating to the Copernican Plan and its variations. But teachers who sought the insights and experiences of others who had preceded them into the world of block periods found little on which to draw.

During the 1995–96 school year, 40 teachers from 10 Seattle–Puget Sound, Washington, area high schools that had already adopted some form of block-period schedule conducted action research studies within their own schools focused on "effective teaching and learning in high school block periods." The purpose of the research was to develop the beginnings of a useful knowledge base about effective teaching and learning in block periods of 80 minutes or more. Four teachers from each participating high school worked together as a research team, and David Marshak, an assistant professor at Seattle University, supported each team as the project coordinator.

During the school year, each research team first articulated its own research question. Then each team developed a number of data collection instruments pertinent to its question. Each team field-tested its instruments, revised them as needed, and employed them with various numbers of teachers, students, and administrators. When the teams had collected their data, each team devoted significant time and energy to considering the data, drawing conclusions and findings as appropriate, and eventually exploring the meanings and implications of what they had learned.

The studies were completed in July 1996; seven are included in this volume. In addition, most of the studies were critiqued by teams of two Puget Sound area high school teachers who themselves teach within a block-period structure. Five of these peer responses appear in this volume, as do comments by the editor about each study.

The following conditions and variables influenced the studies:

- The schools are diverse, ranging from rural to exurban to suburban to central city, and from about 500 students to more than 1,800.

- Most of the schools have unique schedules. Many have only block periods. Others have one or more short-period days each week. Every school has at least 2 days each week of at least 80-minute periods. Some schools have 90-minute periods. Some use 100 minutes. One school has 110-minute periods.

- Each school had its own unique process for exploring and adopting block periods. In each case, the impetus for structural change from short to block periods came *from the school itself,* not from a district or state mandate or initiative.

Chapter 1 presents an analysis of these studies, which suggests the beginnings of a new model of high school for a postindustrial era. Chapter 2 explores the nature of action research
and considers its role both in creating and enacting this new
model of high school. Chapters 3 through 9 present the seven
action research studies at the heart of this project, with critical
commentaries.

The nature and quality of these action research studies is
illustrative of the entire process of transformation now begun
in many high schools in this nation. Each of these teams of
teacher-researchers set off on this journey of action research
with a high level of interest and motivation, good intentions,
and a commitment to professional growth. The members of
each team learned a great deal both about action research and
about teaching and learning in block periods. Yet, none of these
teams had enough time to do all the work that might have
been done productively within their research projects, because
they were all full-time teachers; and in the conventional model
of school, we have almost no structures to support the idea that
teachers can conduct useful research about their own profession.

All of these teacher-researchers, with two exceptions, were
research novices. Even the two exceptions had had only a single previous research experience in their teacher preparation
program. So all of these studies have an intriguing, at times
frustrating, yet always insightful "beginner's mind" quality to
them. All of the studies are flawed and limited in some important ways, yet all of them are very interesting, informative,
and revealing.

The studies can be organized into three categories. The first
three studies—Shorewood, Gig Harbor, and Cedarcrest—focus
on teachers' and students' perceptions and beliefs about what
constitutes effective teaching and learning in block periods.

♦   The **Shorewood High School** study, conducted by David
    Guthrie, Pat Hegarty, Suzanne Louden, and Marian Thom,
    explores teachers' perceptions and beliefs about the kinds
    of teaching and learning activities that are effective in block
    periods. It also looks at the patterns of activities that teach-

ers construct for use in long periods. The study compares teachers' reports about their teaching practice with the perceptions of students about what kinds of teaching they experience within their block-period classes.

♦   The **Gig Harbor High School** study, conducted by Ken Brown, Daniel Dizon, Sherri Patterson, and Derek Sheffield, begins to consider what combinations or sequences of learning activities are perceived by teachers and students to be most effective in block periods. The study, however, provides its most useful insights about teachers' and students' perceptions of effective learning activities regardless of their sequence within a block period.

♦   The **Cedarcrest High School** study, conducted by Feather Alexander, Mark Lovre, Allen Olson, and Anthony L. Smith, explores the use of time in block periods to some extent. Its central findings focus on students' and teachers' perceptions of various teaching and learning activities in the block period in terms of their effectiveness, their engagement of students, the effort that they require from students and teachers, and their frequency of use. The study also explores students' perceptions of teachers' rationales for using various activities.

The next three studies—Tahoma, Decatur, and Lindbergh— focus on particular elements of instruction and curriculum as these are enacted in the block-period schedule.

♦   The **Tahoma High School** study, conducted by Kimberly Allison, Elizabeth Mathewson, Mark Oglesby, and Marianne Winter, begins by devising and defining a central category, *connected learning*. The study explores teachers' and students' perceptions of connected learning, the ways in which block periods can support students' experience of connected learning, and the relationships among connected learning, integrated curriculum, and block periods.

♦   The **Decatur High School** study, conducted by MaryLee Heslop, Rick Hiser, Linda Kristin Reed, and Chris Marquez, explores teachers' reasons for using small groups in block periods and their responses to several key issues of group-based instruction, including the membership of groups, nature of time limits, assignment of roles, and evaluation of student work. The study also presents data about students' perceptions of group work.

♦   The **Lindbergh High School** study, conducted by Helen Bedtelyon, Chris Drape, Jef Rettmann, and Jeannie Wenndorf, considers teachers' and students' perceptions of and beliefs about the uses of new educational technologies, particularly computer-based tools, in the block-period classroom. The study also explores the obstacles to more effective use of technology in the block.

The final study, the **Wilson High School** research, conducted by Mike James, Martin Kelly, Joan M. Sikonia, and Jerry Thorpe, raises the broadscale question of how block periods have improved the quality of student learning at Wilson. It also provides teachers' critiques of the block period in detail and a description of the ways in which Wilson has changed this past year as a result of the new schedule.

# 1

## STEPS TOWARD A NEW MODEL OF HIGH SCHOOL

The action research studies in this volume do not *prove* anything about teaching and learning in block periods. However, these studies do tell us a great deal about what some teachers and students perceive and believe as a result of their several years of experience in block-period classes in American high schools. Taken together as a group of related studies, they offer some steps toward a knowledge base for effective teaching and learning in block periods—*a few steps toward a new idea, a new model, a new paradigm of high school* for what various observers have called a postmodern, postindustrial, information era culture.

The conventional structures of high school are defined by the Committee of Ten subject curriculum and academic departments; short 45–55-minute periods and the Carnegie unit of 120 hours; the comprehensive, tracked high school; lecture, the transmission idea of teaching and learning, and coverage of the subject as the teacher's prime responsibility; and solitary teaching as the norm.

The block period of 80 minutes or more seems to be a slow-acting poison in the bloodstream of the conventional model of high school. Slowly but surely, the block period challenges the continued function of 40–50-minute classes and all of the assumptions and values embedded within them.

The block period seems to serve as both a lever and a stage in the development of a new vision of high school. It is a structural lever, because its length simultaneously invites and impels teachers to change their teaching. A teacher cannot lec-

1

ture for 100 minutes and survive, at least not indefinitely. Long periods persuade many, or perhaps most, teachers to find ways to enrich and complexify their modes of instruction. Long periods also eventually engage many or most teachers in reevaluating their mental models of learning, curriculum, coverage, and assessment.

Some high school teachers already have a rich and complex teaching practice, and the switch to block periods gives them an opportunity to employ their knowledge and skills more fully. Some teachers have a narrower, more conventional teaching practice, yet they jump at the opportunities for change offered by long periods and soon begin to articulate an increasingly diverse and coherent repertoire of teaching and learning activities. Other teachers enter into this work more slowly, often with some or great ambivalence and concern about its high level of demands. Yet, once these teachers begin this effort, they seem more likely to become engaged in what several Puget Sound area teacher-researchers called a "reconceptualization of professional practice." With block periods, teaching in high school sooner or later seems to become a different kind of work for most teachers. In this change process, the longer period provides leverage.

Yet some teachers in block-period structures seem not to change their practice. They continue to lecture or to lead class discussions that are so teacher-centered as to constitute a kind of lecture. And they tend to allow considerable chunks of class time to be used for "hanging out" and homework. The actions of these teachers suggest that the institution of a block-period structure is a necessary step toward a new model of high school but is not sufficient in and of itself. The block period doesn't guarantee change.

Yet, for those who do change, the block period serves as the stage on which teachers enact the more complex and sophisticated repertoire of teaching strategies that block-period instruction can evoke. With 45 minutes, teachers can repeat the same activities day after day. Students may be bored, but most are not likely to rebel. With 45 minutes, teachers who wish to

enact a richly diverse, student-centered pedagogy are re-
strained by the limitations of time.

With 100 minutes, teachers have a much larger space, a
broader and deeper stage, and it is on such a stage that they
create their new practice. And if they don't, students are much
more likely to move beyond boredom into anger and active
rather than passive resistance. Indeed, one not necessarily intended outcome of the block-period schedule that has taken
place in a number of high schools is the choice by teachers who
have refused to adapt to the new model either to leave that
particular school or the teaching profession.

The action research studies conducted within this Seattle–
Puget Sound area project identify nine key elements of
practice, some of which overlap to an extent, that begin to
describe steps toward a new model of high school and high
school teaching.

- ♦ Lecture has a place in the repertoire of the block-
  period teacher, but its use must be limited to its
  appropriate functions; for example, giving directions and explanations or providing enough
  information to set a context for an activity. For
  these functions alone, the Cedarcrest High
  School study suggests that lecture might only be
  employed for about 10% of class time in the
  block period.

- ♦ If the teacher is a skilled and engaging speaker,
  lecture might also be used as one mode of presenting information and ideas. Effective lecturers are usually good storytellers. Information
  embedded in story is often easily remembered,
  because the drama and tension of the story form
  readily engage human beings. But the key to
  this use of lecture is skill. If the teacher is not
  skillful, then she or he needs to limit the use of
  lecture.

  *Lecture is one tool, and only one among many
  modes of teaching. It is not central. Lecture is used
  only for appropriate functions. Storytelling, one kind*

*of lecture, can be a very powerful form of teaching,
because human beings respond to stories.*

♦   In contrast to short periods, block periods require a variety of teaching and learning activities both within each period and over a number
of block periods. Students need to be engaged in
a variety of activities so they can be involved in
their learning throughout the length of the block
period. Students need novelty and change. Using a variety of learning activities also responds
to the learning style diversity among any group
of students and helps all students to be more
fully engaged in the classroom. Variety includes
not only different kinds of activities, such as
discussion, media presentations, role-playing,
lecture, projects, simulations, reading, use of
computer-based technology, research, and so on,
but also includes different grouping structures,
such as whole class, small group, paired, and
individual work.

*Change, variety, and novelty characterize teach-
ing and learning in block periods. A teacher employs
a repertoire of productive activities.*

♦   In addition to an increased variety of teacher-
structured and teacher-led activities, block periods allow—and eventually require—an increase
in the extent to which students are active as
learners and to which they set directions for
their own learning. Block periods provide
enough time for students to explore, question,
engage, initiate, research, develop, build, and
create—in class! Teaching effectively in block
periods requires that teachers continually seek a
constructive balance between the need for them
as adults to guide students and the need for
them to encourage and help students to take
charge of their own learning. As teachers provide students with opportunities for self-

direction, they must also help students develop the skills of self-regulation and organization, which effective self-directed learning requires.

*Students learn to organize and direct their own learning to some significant extent, with the help and guidance of teachers.*

♦ One class structure that works well in block periods both for teacher-led and student-directed activities is the use of cooperative groups. Many of these studies cite group work as a key learning activity in block periods. Students need to be taught how to become skilled group members; they need assistance, support, and boundaries if they are to use group contexts effectively, at least until they require the skills demanded for effective self-regulation.

*Well–structured cooperative group work is one teaching method that works particularly well in block periods, because group work takes time.*

♦ Over time the use of block periods will change the structure of curriculum. Blocks provide time to study material in greater depth. Yet, if some topic is studied in greater depth, some other topic will be omitted, because, for the most part, block periods only rearrange existing class time. As teachers and students study topics in greater depth, and as students become more active as learners, less receivers and more doers, the whole notion of *covering the curriculum* will change. As Ted Sizer has explained, less will become more, as the focus of teachers' concern moves from coverage to student learning.

The Tahoma High School study of connected learning and block periods may very well describe the direction that many block-period high schools will follow in the coming years. According to the Tahoma study, connected learning has context in time and place, connections among various subjects, and an understanding of the importance of both the context and the connections. Block periods give teachers and students the time and space to connect learning—to the students' lives outside of school, to other subjects and disciplines—and to move beyond the content and skills alone to an exploration of the connections themselves. The Tahoma study suggests that block periods may lead to a new understanding of knowledge in high school, where knowledge, to be worthwhile, must have context, connections, meaning, and relevance, both in the present as well as in the future—to students as well as teachers!

*In block-period structures teachers abandon coverage of the curriculum as the key curricular goal and focus their attention on the breadth and depth of student learning, with the understanding that depth of learning and the contextualized quality of knowledge are both important outcomes.*

- Block periods provide the time for more effective utilization of computer-based technologies. As these technologies become increasingly central to our culture, only block-period schools will be able to provide students with the opportunities to master these tools effectively. The Lindbergh High School study provides some initial insights into the nature of this issue and the challenges that teachers face in responding to the demands of technological change.

  *In block periods students have adequate time to use computers for productivity, for research, for communication, and for creativity. Yet all of these functions require time, which only block periods can provide.*

- A key indicator of the success of block period classes is the level of student involvement in the learning. In block periods, student boredom or disengagement cannot be hidden, nor can teacher boredom or ennui. Block periods challenge teachers to enact their larger roles as leaders and coaches, as well as sources of information, and to create classrooms where students are consistently engaged in their learning.

*One key measure of effective teaching in block periods is continuous student involvement in appropriate learning activities.*

♦ The implementation of block periods encourages teachers and students to explore and experiment. For teachers in particular, some level of ongoing experimentation is crucial if they are to develop and maintain a creative edge in their professional work; and teachers must learn to manage the demands of this ongoing experimentation in such a way that they remain vital and engaged, not become overwhelmed and burned out.

*If we are inventing a new model of teaching and learning in high school through the medium of block periods, we must recognize that this work has only begun, and that if we hope to be successful, we must consciously experiment and innovate in a thoughtful and continuous manner.*

♦ Students, adolescents, and young adults can and must enact very different roles in a new model of high school. They are engaged in directing their own learning to some significant extent. They are partners in this process with their teachers, so what they think and feel about their experience in school matters. Students evaluate their learning and the teaching they receive, and they help teachers learn to become more effective. Finally, students are known as individuals by their teachers.

*Students are active shapers of their own learning in some significant ways, and the education they receive is personalized.*

Obviously, these nine elements provide only a sketch of new structures, only steps toward a new model of high school, and only the very beginnings of a knowledge base for effective teaching and learning. Nonetheless, given their origins in the perceptions and beliefs of hundreds of teachers and thousands of students, these elements suggest the possibility of following block-period schedules down a path toward the creation of a very different kind of high school for a new era in our history.

# 2

# COLLABORATIVE ACTION RESEARCH

## WHAT IS COLLABORATIVE ACTION RESEARCH?

Collaborative action research is a methodology through which teachers can formulate a research question that is central to their own professional practice, devise methods of collecting data pertinent to the question, enact the data collection, analyze the data, articulate findings and conclusions that inform their teaching practice, and then change their teaching in ways indicated by the research findings and conclusions.

In one sense, action research is a set of problem-stating and problem-solving procedures. Teacher-researchers identify their own problems and set their own agenda for investigation. As S. Kemmis explains:

> A distinguishing feature of action research is that those affected by planned changes have the primary responsibility for deciding on courses of action which seem likely to lead to improvement, and for evaluating the results of strategies tried out in practice. (Kemmis et al., p. 6)

In another sense, action research engages teachers in articulating theories about their own practice and in evaluating the accuracy and efficacy of these theories. The purpose of this use of theory and related investigation is the improvement of teaching and learning in the learning environment. While knowledge and understanding gained from action research needs to be shared with others, the first purpose of this activity is improvement in teaching and learning. As J. Elliot notes, "It

9

is implicit in the idea of action research that there be some
practical effect or end product to the research; but based on an
increased awareness of what actually happens in the classroom." (Elliot, p. 36)

*Collaborative* action research is a cooperative activity. Teachers work together as colleagues as they conduct an action research project. In the studies documented in this volume,
teacher-researchers worked in teams of four. Beyond the teams'
immediate collaborative activities, most of these teacher-
researchers consciously designed their research so that it
would articulate knowledge and insight regarding teaching in
block periods, sought not only by the teacher-researchers
themselves, but also by a wide range of faculty members in
their schools.

In his definition of collaborative action research, Richard
Sagor brings all of these elements together into a coherent
whole:

> Action research...is conducted by people who want to
> improve their own situation....Action researchers in
> education often focus on three related stages of action:
> initiating action...monitoring and adjusting action...
> [and] evaluating action....Research is defined here as
> any effort toward disciplined inquiry....Action re-
> search can involve a wide array of methods from the
> quantitative and qualitative domains....[Collaborative
> action research] is based on teams of practitioners who
> have common interests and work together to investi-
> gate issues related to those interests. (Sagor, pp. 7-10.)

## How Do You Conduct Collaborative Action Research?

The collaborative action research process includes four
steps. These steps are sketched out below.

## STEP 1: DEFINE THE PROBLEM AND ARTICULATE THE RESEARCH QUESTION

The first step is to define the research problem and articulate the problem as a researchable question.

- *First, collaboratively identify the area of practice, the concern or set of concerns, the topic, or the problem that you want to explore. Then discuss the issue or problem with your colleagues. Use the discussion as a way of determining what problem in practice you all wish to research.* The key element in defining your research problem is your own motivation for learning and improvement. Select a problem about which you care a great deal.

- *Once you have an idea of what the problem is in even a general sense, explore the available literature of research and practice to discover what, if anything, other teachers and researchers have written about this problem.* Divide the documents you find among your colleagues, read them, and report back to each other about whatever you discover. Your reading of the pertinent literature may help you to focus your own research or you may find research instruments that others have devised which you can use, either directly or as models, for your research.

- *State the research problem as clearly as you can. Once the problem is stated it is often helpful to suggest some possible answers or solutions to the problem as hypotheses.* Discuss these hypotheses with your collaborators, considering which one(s) seems most plausible to you. While discussing likely hypotheses is a useful step toward the articulation of a research question, be sure not to jump to any conclusions as a result of this discussion.

- *Once you've developed and considered some hypotheses that address your research problem, develop and state your research question.* The research question is a critical element in the process, because everything that you do from this point on will flow from your question. Be sure to spend enough time discussing, reflecting on, and considering the exact wording of your question, until you reach a point at which all of your collaborators are assured that you have the question you want to answer. As a rule of thumb, you may want to return to your research question on at least three separate occasions, each time stating the intent of your research and reviewing the question's wording to see if you have used precisely the right language.

The teacher-researchers from Tahoma High School, whose study constitutes Chapter 6, knew that they wanted to study "connections that students made in their learning" when they first began their problem definition. Some of their students are in a contained 9th and 10th grade program in which English, social studies, and science courses are integrated in terms of curriculum and some of the teaching-learning activities. They searched the literature for citations pertaining to connections in learning and found very little of substance. This lack of references at first frustrated them and then encouraged them that they had identified a topic where their research might be breaking new ground.

Next they created a term, a category, to identify the phenomenon in which they were interested, *connected learning,* and they engaged their faculty colleagues in defining it, using an exit slip format. Combining the commonalties of the definitions suggested, they created a four-part definition of *connected learning:*

♦ Linking past, present, and future learnings and experiences

♦ Bridging and building concepts and ideas between content areas

- Raising consciousness about the importance of the interconnections
- Raising awareness that life is an intricate web of connections

Working from this definition, they articulated their research questions:

- What is the role of *connected learning* in your own life?
- What is the value of *connected learning* in education?
- What are the strategies for and evidence of *connected learning* in your classroom?

Of course, all of these activities required many hours of team conversations, individual and collective writing of drafts of the definition and research questions, review of individual work by colleagues, and collective agreement about the final forms of the definition and research questions. None of this work was easy, but based on the researchers' reports, almost all of it was interesting, challenging, highly engaging, and rewarding.

## STEP 2: DEVELOP THE RESEARCH INSTRUMENTS

- *The next step in the research process is to select, find, and develop research instruments that will help you to acquire the desired data to answer your research questions.* You may want to use existing instruments that evaluate students' work; for example, portfolios, writing assessments, rubric-based performance assessments, or standardized tests. Or you may want to create a new method of assessing student work that responds directly to your research question.

  You may want to create research instruments that generate data based on your direct observation in a classroom or other setting or on a videotaping of a classroom or other setting. For this, you'll need to develop an observation protocol, which is a set of criteria for organizing and expressing your observations.

You may want to create research instruments that generate data about what teachers and students perceive and believe, for example, a survey or an interview protocol.

You may find research instruments that you can apply for your own use when you search the relevant literature. You may be able to employ such an instrument as is or with some modification to make it fit your question more specifically.

♦ *Once you have developed your research instrument(s), be sure to pilot it with a small number of respondents or data sources.* This pilot will allow you to assess whether or not the instrument(s) actually will generate the kinds of data that you are seeking. In light of the pilot, make any revisions needed to the instrument(s). If you are not certain about the success of your revisions, you'll need to test out the revised instrument(s). Continue this process of evaluation until your research instrument(s) works effectively to generate exactly the kind of data that you seek.

The teacher-researchers from Decatur High School, whose study constitutes Chapter 7, articulated the following research question: *What does group work look like in the 100-minute period?*

Their next step involved the design of the research instruments that they would use to describe the nature of group work in the 100-minute class period at Decatur. After much discussion, they decided to use three methods of data collection, and they developed an appropriate instrument for each.

♦ A teacher interview to determine each teacher's description of group work within a teacher's classroom, with each interview guided by an interview protocol;

+ A classroom observation of each interviewed teacher's 100-minute class during a time when students were engaged in group work, with each observation guided by an observation protocol; and

+ A survey of students enrolled in the classes observed to assess student attitudes toward group work and activities in the classroom. (All three instruments are included in Chapter 7.)

Initially each member of the research team observed and interviewed another member of the team. This activity allowed the Decatur researchers to test and improve their first two data collection instruments. They also conducted a small pilot of their student survey and made some adjustments in its language based on the pilot's results.

## STEP 3: COLLECT DATA, ORGANIZE AND ANALYZE DATA, ARTICULATE FINDINGS, AND DRAW CONCLUSIONS

+ *The next step is to enact your various research instruments and gather pertinent data.* In using research instruments, you'll want to consider a range of variables that may affect the nature of the data collected, such as day of the week, time of day, proximity to school vacations, and so on. For most research questions, you'll want to gather data at times and in places that are typical and ordinary, unless, of course, you are researching a phenomenon that is unusual or extraordinary.

+ *Once you have gathered your data, the next step is to organize it into usable forms.* Test scores and rubric scores need to be tabulated and categorized. Survey responses need to be categorized and tabulated. Observation data need to be coded and tabulated, as do interview data.

If these kinds of data organization and interpretation are new to you, you'll want to study some of the books listed at the end of this chapter, which discuss data analysis in more detail.

♦ *When you have organized your data, the next step is to examine it for findings and to develop and articulate your conclusions.* In this context, a finding is a result described by the data. A conclusion is an explanation or understanding that results from a finding.

The teacher-researchers from Lindbergh High School, whose study constitutes Chapter 7, investigated the use of technology, particularly computers, in block periods. They developed and enacted a faculty survey, a student survey, and an "expert" interview.

They organized their survey data into percentage categories (e.g., 67% of students surveyed said using technology helped them to learn better), which were findings, and articulated a set of thematic conclusions (e.g., most students like to use technology in the classroom).

Another example of a finding was that 63% of the teachers reported *teacher preparation* as their primary use of technology. From this finding the researchers drew the conclusion that a majority of teachers at Lindbergh have not yet integrated the use of technology into their regular teaching practice in the classroom.

## STEP 4: CREATE AN ACTION PLAN AND ENACT IT

♦ *Once you have articulated findings and developed conclusions, the final step in the action research process is to generate an action plan based on your conclusions and to put its elements into effect.* The purpose of action research is to improve teaching and learning. It is at this step in the process that you make the improvements in your teaching, guided by the conclusions you have drawn from your research.

The teacher-researchers from Shorewood High School, whose study constitutes Chapter 3, included the following in their action plan:

It is obvious that our sense of what happens in the block-period classroom is sometimes quite different from that of our students, and this knowledge must serve as a vehicle to have us reconsider how we are delivering education, as well as how we are being perceived by those who sit in our classrooms....One way to gain this deeper understanding would be to create two new instruments to gauge student perceptions. A modified student log, used in concert with the teacher activity log, would help us see where the discrepancies are in our various perceptions. It would also be useful to create a student interview form, much like the one used with teachers. This would be used in conjunction with the teachers' form. In addition to this providing greater depth to our investigations, it would also create a more controlled set of data, as we could be sure that we were actually talking about the same circumstances when we compared data from the different instruments.

The teacher-researchers from Gig Harbor High School, whose study constitutes Chapter 4, included the following in their action plan:

Our results have confirmed a suspicion we already held: Lecture, as the primary educational method in the classroom, is ineffective. Even though we already knew this, it is comforting to have data from our own school in support of this conclusion. However, our results have revealed something new to all of us, and that is the importance of lecture-like explanation and setup so students are clear about their goal in a project or group activity. We intend to spend more time preparing our introductions to student-centered activities by incorporating engaging sets and presenting students with written directions. We decided also that if we have the time, it is helpful to rehearse the directions with another teacher to receive feedback regarding clarity.

We have also been reminded of the importance of variety in 100 minutes. In our planning, we intend to "mix it up," to shift gears from teacher-centered activities to student-centered ones in the same period. Also, we plan to extend the results somewhat to encourage ourselves to employ different kinds of evaluative methods. These can include writing, speeches, visual/poster-like projects, dramatic reenactments, and so on. This is the most significant realization of our research, the key role of variety. And this is the criterion we will use to evaluate our own teaching in the future.

## STEP 5: REPORTING RESULTS

In *How to Conduct Collaborative Action Research*, Sagor identifies another step in the action research process: reporting results. Sagor argues that teacher-researchers need to report their results to their colleagues and the larger educational community through presentation and publication. This endeavor is worth the additional effort, he believes, for these reasons:

To break the norm of isolation common in many schools and encourage teacher-researchers to share their work with their immediate peers;

To include active teachers among those who contribute significantly to the profession's knowledge base about teaching and learning; and

To gain for teachers a stronger role in articulating what constitutes effective teaching and learning in their own schools.

## PRACTICAL RESOURCES

This section has provided only a sketch of the collaborative action research process. For more detailed information, you can review these resources:

Sagor, R. *How to Conduct Collaborative Action Research.* Alexandria, VA: ASCD, 1992.

Calhoun, E.F. *How to Use Action Research in the Self-Renewing School.* Alexandria VA: ASCD.

Hubbard, R.S. and B. Miller Power. *The Art of Classroom Inquiry: A Handbook for Teacher-Researchers.* Portsmouth, NH: Heinemann.

Oja, S.N. and L. Smulyan. *Collaborative Action Research: A Developmental Approach.* London: Falmer Press, 1989.

Stringer, E.T. Action Research: A Handbook for Practitioners. Thousand Oaks, CA: Sage Publications, 1996.

# WHAT DO TEACHERS SAY ABOUT CONDUCTING COLLABORATIVE ACTION RESEARCH?

*Feather Alexander, a teacher at Cedarcrest High School:*

Collaborative action research forced me, from the beginning, to focus, collect, and actually record my thoughts on what I thought to be effective, and to actually look at those practices in my school and in my classroom and ask myself if those practices I observed and studied matched my ideals of effective teaching and learning. Keeping records and applying my observations to the formulation of research questions helped me to put reflection into action—to utilize reflection to improve teaching and learning.

*Kimberly Allison, Liz Mathewson, and Marianne Winter, teachers at Tahoma High School:*

We certainly developed a first name relationship with ambiguity as we wrestled with several amorphous ideas before we finally settled on a focus. Even with a focus of connected learning, we stumbled through the process as novice researchers. The value of this was time for teacher talk, which, while sometimes frustrating, was extremely valuable. The discussions related to real-life classroom problems and issues, and they reinforced the belief that teachers need time to come together for purposeful and meaningful discourse....Collaborative action research forced us to become academic researchers, taking the cerebral aspects of research and making them relevant to our everyday lives as teachers.

*Mark Lovre, a teacher at Cedarcrest High School:*

The biggest benefit of action research was in doing it. The process of developing a research question forced me to focus on my teaching, as well as the learning that was happening in my classroom. The process also allowed me multiple opportunities to see how other teachers thought about learning and teaching and how they worked.... The research ranges from quantitative to very conversational, but all is couched in a format that lends itself to immediate application in the classroom.

*Kristi Noren, a teacher at Foster High School in Tukwila, Washington:*

The benefits: the research is practical, applying to our daily tasks as teachers. The chance to work cooperatively with peers, to learn from each other, synthesize ideas about instruction, and so on....Lots of learning, "food for thought," new questions and viewpoints.... Learning the process of action research through doing, though frustrating at times, was a good learning experience. Our learning was a more worthwhile outcome than our project....Limitations: forming a question that was not too broad and that was research-friendly....Finding team time to work. None of our team members had experience with research, so we often felt that we were stumbling in the dark. Data analysis was more time consuming than we anticipated. We had difficulty deciding the most useful and significant ways to look our data.

*Chris Drape, a teacher at Lindbergh High School:*

Collaborative action research was an opportunity to work with others directly....As teachers we are more creative, insightful, and even productive as a group than we could be as individuals. By reflecting and problem posing and solving with others, we get at ideas, questions, and possible answers that we would not necessarily come to on our own. Given the benefits, it remains hard to coordinate with everyone at times. We still work in a system that is very individualized, and it can be hard to maintain the energy necessary to carry a project to completion.

*Allen Olsen, a teacher at Cedarcrest High School:*

The major benefit that I perceived was the information that we were able to gather from different constituents: teachers, students, and administrators. It was amazing how close the opinions of these three groups were to each other....Without the processes involved in action research, the information we gathered would have been much less meaningful to me personally. It is really the process, not so much the results, which allow for learning and growth. Yet too often in education we allow one group of people to do the research and distribute the results to others who are supposed to somehow incorporate the results into their practice....The research can be easily discounted as disconnected from practice. Since action research is research conducted by practitioners, it holds more meaning for them in general.

*Jeannie Wenndorf, a teacher at Lindbergh High School:*

Benefits: opportunities to have meaningful interaction with colleagues....I learned much from them about their challenges in the classroom and creative solutions they had regarding some of my challenges....Focused time to look at my own teaching. We studied the use of technology in the classroom. I was able to analyze my own use of technology, and I have made different choices in that area this year, applying what I learned from our action research study....Opportunity to do meaningful work that goes beyond the classroom. Our action research helped me, and it's available to other teachers so they might benefit as well. Contributing to the greater body of knowledge regarding teaching and learning provides meaning to my teaching career....The action research model provides a tool for self-evaluation....Limitations: We began the research with some preconceived notions of what our conclusions would be. It was difficult to create an objective way to collect and analyze data....Our results seemed a bit insignificant. Our data supported what we already believed to be true. It seems our research benefited us but not so much the audience.

*Anthony L. Smith, a counselor at Cedarcrest High School:*

The notion of spending a concentrated amount of time in formulating the research question was helpful to the eventual outcome of the study and helped us pinpoint possible concerns with the integrity of the research....This type of research is a realistic compromise between more rigorously objective research, with its concerns for validity and reliability, and largely subjective and personal judgments about educational issues.

*Feather Alexander:*

Collaborative research, by definition, does not allow for isolated study. The group processes which evolved were some of the most meaningful experiences in the study. Our team was forced to come together, to step out of our own fragmented teaching lives, to open doors of communication and understanding across disciplines, and to come up with a collective vision of our study. Throughout the process we struggled for consensus, challenged each other's views, and through frustration, we came out of this experience with a better understanding of teaching, learning, and, most importantly, each other. We created a document which reflected ideas which were important to all of us. Key to the whole process was that our study had not been done to sit on a shelf, to be pondered by scholars, but it had been written by us for our uses in recognizing effective teaching and in planning for improvement. Because of the personal relevance, I felt this to be a truly powerful experience.

## WHY CONNECT ACTION RESEARCH AND BLOCK-PERIOD STRUCTURES?

The connection between collaborative action research and block-period structures is a natural one. In the past, critics outside the high school have called for change in the way that high schools operate. And many or most high school teachers have questioned the validity and utility of such criticism from outsiders, from those who don't have the day-to-day experience of teaching adolescents in an American high school.

As Allen Olsen noted earlier:

> ...Too often in education we allow one group of people to do the research and distribute the results to others who are supposed to somehow incorporate the results into their practice....The research can be easily discounted as disconnected from practice. Since action research is research conducted by practitioners, it holds more meaning for them in general.

Teachers conduct collaborative action research. Its practice may empower teachers to take some significant measure of control in defining the ways in which their own work and workplace will change in conjunction with the larger social and cultural transformation that we are clearly experiencing both in America and throughout the world. As Parker Palmer notes, "in such a collaborative undertaking (of action research), people empower one another....(They) define problems and gather facts so that research becomes a form of empowerment and action." (Palmer, pp. 3–4.) And other teachers can't so easily ignore or discredit research conducted by their colleagues.

Collaborative action research gives teachers a method through which they can explore the uses of block-period structures and develop and refine both these new structures and their teaching practices within these contexts. Collaborative action research is a way of discovering how to teach more effectively for the purpose of generating student learning and growth, how to implement innovation, and how to demonstrate the validity of both innovations and fruitful traditional methods to colleagues, administrators, parents, and the public at large.

## SOME ACTION RESEARCH QUESTIONS AND ANSWERS

The following are some of the questions teachers ask about action research, and a practical response to each question.

### HOW DOES ACTION RESEARCH DIFFER FROM CONVENTIONAL ACADEMIC RESEARCH?

The purpose of conventional academic research most often is to develop and articulate knowledge. In education, such knowledge is usually derived from examination of a particular setting or settings, but the researcher's intent is to develop knowledge not only about the particular setting examined but about all similar settings. This quality of knowledge is called *generalizability*, "the applicability of findings to settings and contexts different from the one in which they were originally obtained." (Sagor, p. 28.)

Action research, in contrast, is focused on identifying problems of practice and solving problems and improving practice. The action researcher can ignore the issue of generalizability, because the action researcher does not make any claims about the applicability of the researcher's findings to settings other than the researcher's own.

The editor of this volume does make some tentative larger claims based on the action research studies included here, as well as several others. But these claims are based on 10 separate action research studies conducted in 10 separate schools in several different kinds of communities across the Seattle–Puget Sound area. So, these claims of generalizability are based not on a single study, but on many studies. In addition, the claims are stated largely as hypotheses or as tentative conclusions based on the available data. And certainly all of these conclusions demand far more study.

## CAN TEACHERS REALLY DO RESEARCH?

Yes, absolutely! Teachers have conducted productive action research for decades. The teachers in this project all had some constructive role in conducting the research described in the ensuing chapters.

If you want to conduct action research in your own classroom or school, you can find guidance in the resources listed above under Practical Resources.

Perhaps the greatest value of collaborative action research—and its saving grace when the research becomes challenging—is that teachers work together. They learn together, they help each other, they struggle together, and they succeed together.

## HOW DO TEACHERS FIND TIME FOR RESEARCH? HOW MUCH TIME DOES AN ACTION RESEARCH STUDY REQUIRE?

Time is the greatest scarcity for teachers in American schools today. Finding time to conduct action research is a challenge. The teachers who conducted the studies in this volume received a small stipend of several hundred dollars each from a grant. Yet, the money was clearly a lesser motivation for their work. Yes, it was a recognition of the value and professional quality of their endeavor—in our society professionals are paid for their efforts—but the far greater motivation and source of rewards for these teachers was the research effort itself, both the process and the results.

So how do teachers find time? Perhaps the most effective way to find time is to structure the collaborative action research effort as the teacher's professional development activity for a period of time. Most high schools have a structure of staff or professional development these days, which involves some arrangement of half days, contractual or separately paid after-school time, funding for conferences and workshops, professional release days, and various other work opportunities or contexts. Because one of the greatest values of collaborative action research is its effect as professional development for the teacher-researchers, directing a school's staff development time and budget toward this kind of activity, whether for one small group of teachers, a department, or even an entire faculty, if all or even most of the teachers are so motivated, would be a very productive use of school or district resources.

Of course, another model is the one employed in this project. Find some grant-funding, recruit some teachers who want to conduct action research, and use the funding as a way to support participation.

How much time is needed to conduct a study? Of course, that will vary widely, depending on the nature and size of the research and the skills and group process of the researchers. The research groups from this project engaged most of their teacher-researchers in several dozen hours of work over the course of the entire school year, with a chunk of that time coming after the close of school in June.

## HOW DO YOU SELECT THE RIGHT TOPIC OR ISSUE TO EXPLORE THROUGH ACTION RESEARCH?

The most important issue in the selection of an action research topic or question is *how much you want to know the answer*. The more you want to know, the more energy you'll devote to finding out.

If you are collaborating in your research endeavor, you may be able to find a colleague(s) who has exactly the same question that you do. This is ideal. If this is not the case, then you'll either need to negotiate a common question or agree to pursue parallel or related research together.

## WHAT'S THE DIFFERENCE BETWEEN QUANTITATIVE AND QUALITATIVE RESEARCH? WHICH SHOULD YOU USE, AND WHEN?

Quantitative research involves the generation and manipulation of data that can be enumerated in some way. The data can be expressed as quantities, hence the name.

Qualitative research focuses on data that are primarily descriptive. The data can be expressed as qualities.

In action research you can use either quantitative or qualitative approaches, or both. The issue is not which approach to use, but what is your research question and what kinds of data will provide you with the best answers to your question.

For example, if you want to know what students think and feel about the writing instruction that they receive in block periods, you'll need to gather descriptive responses, which will be qualitative in character.

If you want to measure the improvement of students' writing skills in block periods, as assessed by a rubric-scored direct writing assessment, then you will generate a set of quantitative data.

## WHAT DO VALIDITY AND RELIABILITY MEAN?

In this context, validity means that the data do in fact measure what the researcher says they measure. For example, data from student surveys about the effectiveness of block periods for learning can be valid in relation to a research question about students' perceptions or beliefs about the value of block periods. But the same kind of data from student surveys are not likely to be valid in relation to a question about students' abilities to solve word problems in Integrated Math I (unless the students have had a good deal of experience in evaluating their own problem-solving skills in relation to some kind of pertinent rubric, and thus their perceptions do, in fact, accurately reflect their levels of skill).

Reliability, in this context, refers to the ability of research instruments to produce accurate data. A reliable research instrument will generate roughly the same range of data if administered to the same population, or a similar population, at different times. For example, if a survey were to generate wildly different responses from similar populations of teachers, without any apparent reasons for such differences, there may be some element in the language or structure of the survey itself that makes it unreliable. However, using qualitative instruments, you can get greatly different responses at different times, or from similar but different populations, because the conditions or events that respondents are experiencing are very different.

Sagor suggests three questions for action researchers to apply in relation to the issues of validity and reliability:

1. Do the instruments and methods we plan to use measure what we claim they do?

2. Do the instruments and methods we plan to use accurately measure the phenomena we are studying?

3. Will a skeptic be convinced by the weight of the data we amass? (Sagor, p. 31.)

## WHY DO INEXPERIENCED ACTION RESEARCHERS MAKE ERRORS? WHAT HAPPENS IF YOU MAKE ERRORS?

All beginning action researchers make errors, because action research is a complex and challenging endeavor without a clear set of rules for every situation. This book and others can give you a set of procedures that will help you get underway, but you'll inevitably come to places in the research process where you and your collaborators will need to make judgments.

Often you'll make good judgments. Sometimes you'll make errors. Everybody does. What you need to do with errors is first recognize them, then learn from them whatever you can, and then, to the extent possible, remedy them.

Each of the studies in this volume includes some errors. If the teacher-researchers who conducted these studies were to enact them again, they'd be likely to rectify most or all of these errors. And then they might come to new and even more challenging places in the research, where they might make a new error or two.

## IS ACTION RESEARCH A SINGLE ACTIVITY OR A CYCLE OF STUDY AND INNOVATION, FOLLOWED BY MORE STUDY?

Action research can be a single sequence of study: identify the problem, frame the question, develop the instrument, gather the data, develop the findings and conclusions, generate the action plan, and put it into operation.

Action research can also be recursive or cyclical. In this pattern, the researchers conduct the study up to the point of enacting the action plan, as noted above. Instead of stopping at this point, the researchers then apply their instrument(s) to gather data about the solutions they have put into operation, analyze the data, and so on. In this way, the action research process can be used as an ongoing means of improvement and refinement of teaching activities, school structures, and so on.

## THE STUDIES IN THIS PROJECT SEEMED TO FOCUS ON THE WHOLE SCHOOL. SHOULD I FOCUS ON THE WHOLE SCHOOL OR ON MY OWN CLASSROOM?

All of the research teams in this project consciously chose to use this opportunity to study issues or questions of schoolwide significance. This was not required in any way by the grant or research coordinator. Rather, it was a decision by the researchers to conduct studies that would have the most value not only to themselves but also to the greatest number of their faculty colleagues.

This schoolwide focus is certainly appropriate for action research, but so is a focus on a particular classroom(s), course, curriculum, program, unit, teaching method, or even a particular lesson. Any and every element of teaching practice as well as school function can be examined productively through the action research methodology.

## BIBLIOGRAPHY

Elliot, J. (1982). "Action research: A framework for self-evaluation in schools." Working Paper No. 1, *Teacher-Pupil Interaction and the Quality of Learning*. London: Schools Council (mimeo).

Kemmis, S. et al. (1982). *The Action-Research Planner*. 2nd ed. Victoria: Deakin University Press.

Palmer, P. (1974). *Action Research: A New Style of Politics in Education*. Boston: Institute for Responsive Education.

Sagor, R. (1992) *How to Conduct Collaborative Action Research*. Alexandria VA: Association for Supervision and Curriculum Development.

# 3

# SHOREWOOD HIGH SCHOOL
## CHANGES IN TEACHING STRATEGIES AS A RESULT OF THE BLOCK PERIOD

David Guthrie, Pat Hegarty
Suzanne Louden, Marian Thom

### SCHOOL PORTRAIT AND INTRODUCTION

Shorewood High School is a comprehensive high school composed of grades 9 through 12 with an enrollment of 1,515 students. It is one of two high schools in the Shoreline district, serving the inhabitants of the west side of Shoreline, the fourth largest city in King County, Washington. Approximately 90% of Shorewood students go on to further schooling, with 46% enrolling in 4-year colleges and universities. About 23% of the students are persons of color.

A newly incorporated city, Shoreline is a community directly north of Seattle that covers 12 square miles and is home to 50,352 people. The economy is based on service and commercial activities.

Shorewood High School has just completed its second full year of operating on what is known as the ABC schedule:

4 days of three 100-minute periods ("A" days and "B" days) and 1 day of 50-minute periods ("C" days).

In the late 1980s, Shorewood faculty expressed an interest in exploring alternative schedules. Summer collaboration time was encouraged by the administration, with files of information collected regarding what was happening elsewhere in the country. The general feeling was that the staff and students functioned under far too fast a pace and that we were trapped in a cycle of offering *more* each year with *less* time to do quality work and to establish meaningful connections with our students. By the fall of the 1992–93 school year, new principal Rick Robbins asked for volunteers to explore alternative schedule options. Six faculty members from a variety of departments, along with three actively involved parents, committed to investigating the options and reporting back to the staff. The entire process consumed two complete school years, with Shorewood's version of a block-period schedule first enacted in the fall of the 1994–95 school year.

The work of the Alternative Schedule Committee was one of the most positive, well-received staff efforts of the past several years. Committee members met approximately every 2 weeks, all volunteering their time after school, and agreed to explore every possible option, including year-round schools, rotating modular plans, trimesters, and so on. The overriding goal of the staff was to find a schedule that would improve the quality of instruction and "slow things down" for everyone. At regular intervals during the committee's exploratory process, the group reported to the staff, always taking time to listen carefully to the ideas and concerns of those in the various departments.

The committee was diligent in pursuit of ideas, making an effort to do a national search in order to become familiar with as many innovations as possible. Committee members made phone calls, visited other schools, had personal conferences, requested copies of materials, and gradually reworked and refined many different plans to come up with three options for the entire staff to consider. Through the entire process, the goal of the committee was to keep in very close touch with our school community in order to build an alternative schedule reflecting the values of all Shorewood stakeholders: students, parents, teachers, support staff, administrators, and other community members. In retrospect, this proved to be an extremely valuable philosophy.

Shortly into the second semester of the 1993–94 school year, the committee presented three different plans to the faculty for discussion and study. Prior to that presentation (and consistently until the ultimate decision was made), the team revisited the guidelines under which the alternative schedule search had operated and made every effort to validate the reasons for having presented each of the three possible schedules. Following that initial presentation, the staff rotated through smaller groups headed by "specialist" team members, each one exploring in further detail the advantages and disadvantages of each option. Then, rather than force a hasty vote on the three plans, the committee and staff opted to reconvene a few weeks later, after having had time to discuss the options informally. That, too, proved to be a prudent move. Students, staff, and the community were so genuinely interested in making a change that lots of healthy discussion followed, usually informally. Committee members kept an "ear to the ground" for concerns, continued to meet regularly, and eventually refined the original plans in preparation for the second all-staff–community consideration.

By early spring of 1994, one of the three original plans had been eliminated for lack of strong support. The two remaining plans were quite different, one being a trimester option and the other being a two-semester plan. Their common characteristic was that each would offer fewer instructional periods per day with each period being considerably longer. At that point the committee began to ask for some real sense of commitment to either of the two plans and developed several instruments to "take the pulse" of the various departments, in particular. Mailings about the plans were also sent out to parents, and several informational meetings were held to be sure that the entire community had a chance to evaluate what was being proposed.

Concerning the various departments of the school, it had been clear from the onset of the alternative schedule search that teachers of the lab classes (science, art, Home and Family Living) were overwhelmingly in favor of longer periods. Teachers of social studies, English, foreign languages, and other communication-based classes were typically quite receptive to the idea. Far less convinced were the math teachers, the physical education department, and the music department. The committee accordingly made a maximal effort to listen to the concerns of teachers in the three latter departments and to put them in touch with colleagues in other schools who were successfully teaching with an alternative schedule. All staff realized that whatever the intensity of individual commitment to a new plan, everyone would benefit from re-training and re-thinking what had always been done. At one faculty meeting, a visiting team of teachers from Gig Harbor High School shared experiences about their teaching in block periods and answered questions.

Finally, as the process continued, the committee began asking for a show of "fists of five" to indicate enthusiasm for the plans. (Five fingers in the air indicated an overwhelming "Let's get on with it" support and a closed fist represented an "I'm not in favor and won't cooperate willingly" feeling. Somewhere in between were those who were unconvinced, had some reservations, or were ready to jump in and needed only a nudge.) Gradually, the trimester plan seemed to lose favor, leaving a two-semester, three-period day as the most likely choice.

By that time, all of the committee members were absolutely convinced that an alternative schedule could be in place by the fall of 1994. The goal was to adopt a plan that would be supported by as many staff, students, and community members as possible. The final vote occurred in the late spring of 1994, with more than 90% of the Shorewood faculty voting in favor of starting the plan in the fall 1994–95 school year. By that time, many parents were also enthusiastic about the plan, and word spread throughout the community that Shorewood was about to try something new that would benefit kids. That was the overriding message we tried to spread throughout the community.

One of the major concerns that had been expressed consistently throughout the process was that these models found faculty seeing students fewer times in a week. One of the primary goals, however, had been to connect teachers more *closely* to students through more quality contact time. Accordingly, the committee refined the plan that came to be known as the ABC schedule, with A and B days of three 100-minute periods and a C day of six 50-minute periods. The advantage of such a schedule was that each student would see each teacher three times a week.

We have now completed two entire years under the ABC schedule, and the general consensus is that almost no one would ever willingly return to the previous six classes per day. Certainly, there are those who still have reservations about the efficacy of long periods. The lack of a planning period for teachers on alternate days continues to be a problem. C days are generally frustrating for everyone because they seem extremely rushed, inefficient, and exhausting, and although few really like them, there is agreement that we do need the third contact day each week. The administration feels strongly that before tinkering further with the schedule, we need to make every effort to live with the plan as set up, as it certainly has represented the very best collaboration of all members of the Shorewood community.

At the outset of our implementation of this block-period schedule, two major concerns emerged at Shorewood. The first had to do with the concern of not seeing our students every day. There has been, and there still persists, the feeling among some of the faculty that daily contact is tremendously important in terms of tracking our students' progress. For some teachers this concern has been especially troubling when we consider the plight of students who are "at risk." The line of thinking in some core subject areas is that the simple day-to-day tasks that these students often overlook—daily attendance, bringing appropriate materials to class, reading in preparation for class—are greater problems when the teacher cannot encourage the student to take care of these basics each and every day. Further, this issue was most salient in classes where performance is an essential part of the curriculum. In many music classes, for example, a number of our teachers still feel that the level of performance that students display has diminished as a result of not having daily contact with the instrument and the instructor.

Yet another concern, that at this writing has more or less subsided, was the STAR period. From the very beginning, it was not at all clear how exactly we would hold students accountable for their whereabouts during this relatively free period. Initially, we wanted to promote a college campus-like feeling at Shorewood for that 25-minute period each day. Students would be free to take care of their business, at their diligent leisure, in a variety of settings across campus. At the same time, a sizable segment of the staff was adamant about not wanting the equivalent of another prep period: Nobody wanted an assigned group of students that they alone would be responsible for.

STAR began, then, as an open time during which students would work independently. Unfortunately, a significant number of students chose to wander the campus every day rather than commit to working, and, as a result, a system of accountability—STAR cards—was introduced for all students. Students, especially seniors, were less than happy about this change, as evidenced in their comments at a student–faculty forum organized by the committee that put together the STAR card proposal. In addition, parents were concerned that the revised process necessitated students getting a separate card for library use, as they feared it would lessen student access to the library during STAR. Nevertheless, this system has continued, with a great degree of success and very little rancor.

## RESEARCH METHODOLOGY

Our work began with a presentation to the faculty about action research. Our task was to explain the purpose of action research as it relates to the study of the block-period schedule.

This done, we conducted a quick survey of the staff in which each faculty member was given a slip of paper and asked to identify two areas of concern surrounding teaching and learning in the block-period classroom (see Appendix 3.1).

Based on the teachers' responses we identified these eight possible research questions:

- How has the block-period schedule affected special needs students at Shorewood?
- In what ways has teaching in block periods changed instructional strategies/styles?
- What are the implications of combining the traditional C schedule (50-minute period), with the A/B format?
- Has the block period changed the quality of human interactions at Shorewood?
- Does the block-period schedule foster greater student responsibility?
- Has the staff been adequately prepared and supported in moving from the traditional schedule to the new schedule?
- What implications does this change in schedule present for homework?
- Are there instructional issues that are problematic for some departments, but not for others? What are they?

Once we identified these questions, we conducted a "value voting" exercise with the faculty in an attempt to gain further "buy in" on the final research question. Each of the questions was posted on its own piece of newsprint. Having been allocated five red sticker dots, each faculty member was instructed to place his or her dots on the questions that he or she valued most highly. However, a number of people called for a ninth question: "Does a block-period schedule lead to an increase in learning?" Question 9 emerged as the clear winner, with question 2 running a close second.

We realized, of course, that "Does a block-period schedule lead to an increase in learning?" was much too broad a question for us to cover, and our advisor David Marshak agreed. With his assistance, we chose to go with a modified version of question 2: *How have teaching techniques and strategies changed as a result of block periods, and what does this tell us about teacher values regarding what leads to learning?* This revised query covered the faculty's original concerns, while the added question also helped respond to their interest in addressing learning. The faculty accepted this revision, giving their blessing to our research question.

The formal research process began, once again, with our colleagues, who, at a faculty meeting, responded to yet another survey related to our research project (see Appendix 3.2). In this case, our goal was twofold. First, we hoped to get a sense from the faculty which teaching practices they found most useful in the 100-minute period format. Given a list of 10 different instructional strategies, we asked our colleagues to rate each strategy on a scale of 1 to 5. In this case, a score of 5 indicated that this strategy was deemed highly effective, whereas a score of 1 indicated that the respondent felt the strategy was not terribly effective in the block-period classroom.

Our second goal in this survey was to invite teachers to become active participants in the research. At the bottom of the instrument, we asked that 20 teachers volunteer to participate in two other activities: the teaching activity log and the informal interview. Having identified the 20 teachers who agreed to participate, we then created the teaching activity log (see Appendix 3.4). This log asked the teacher to choose one class and, over the course of 1 week, record the activities that the class went through each day that week. In asking this, we hoped that the teacher would identify the activity from the category list provided and indicate how much time was spent on each activity.

The research team also elicited volunteers for the interviews (see Appendix 3.5), divided up this group of respondents, and set aside some time to interview each teacher about the teacher's beliefs and practices. The five questions all revolved around issues of instructional practices and student learning. Our hope was to ascertain the extent to which teacher comments about strategies and values matched what they wrote on the classroom activity logs.

Our final research instrument was a survey distributed randomly to 19 Shorewood students, grades 9 through 12 (see Appendix 3.6). Again, the questions revolved around issues of instructional practices and student learning, and our hope was to see to what degree teacher comments and classroom activity logs were mirrored in student responses. The survey asked students to, "Mark the response that correctly identifies the percentage of time you spend during *an average week* on the following activities in your third period class," with responses ranging from "most of the time" (a score of 1) to "hardly ever" (a score of 5). It is important to note that the students who completed this survey were not necessarily students of the teachers who participated in the study. In fact, we made no attempt to make this match, a concern addressed later in this report.

## FINDINGS AND ANALYSIS

### RATING INSTRUCTIONAL ACTIVITIES (APPENDICES 3.2 AND 3.3)

Thirty faculty members responded to the instrument. On this instrument, a score of 5 indicated that a strategy was deemed highly effective in the block-period class, as compared to the same strategy in the traditional class period, while a score of 1 indicated that the respondent felt the strategy was not terribly effective in the block-period classroom.

The most revealing outcome of the results is that very few responses fell within the lowest scores of 1 and 2. Those responses that were 1 and 2 were related to teachers' concerns about students not retaining what they had practiced as a result of not having daily teacher contact.

A simple scanning of the data reveals a high percentage of respondents feeling that class discussion, library time, group work, independent work, student presentations, use of technology, and simulations are all strategies that appear to work better in the 100-minute period than in the short period. On the other hand, lecturing gets a rather ho-hum rating.

## THE TEACHING ACTIVITY LOG (APPENDIX 3.4)

In interpreting and evaluating the results of this log-keeping, we organized our data so that we could categorize it as to (1) variety of activities used, (2) activities used in A/B days as compared with C days, and (3) patterns of activities used.

### VARIETY

The responding teachers all mentioned using some type of activity that could be categorized as:

- Group work
- Demonstration
- Discussion/class participation
- Guided practice
- Multimedia
- Independent work
- Lab work

### A/B DAYS COMPARED WITH C DAYS

As previously mentioned, most teachers felt far more rushed when teaching in the traditional 55-minute periods and tended to use C days more for *student project presentations, quizzes and tests,* or *multimedia use.* (One issue that the faculty tried to address very soon after we began using the long periods was that too many teachers chose to give tests and quizzes on the C days, thus creating anxiety for students who might end up with multiple tests on one day. Parents and students were quick to express their frustration with this, and we discussed it in faculty meetings and made every effort to correct the situation.)

## PATTERNS OF ACTIVITIES

We were interested in knowing whether the block periods changed patterns dramatically. Some veteran teachers in particular pointed out that in the long periods they actually did exactly what they used to do in the shorter periods, recognizing the need for variety, but they had far more time to develop each step. For example, several teachers recorded *discussion* followed by either *group or independent work*, or *demonstration* followed by *lab work*. Some teachers were aware of being better able to address the issue of learning styles/multiple intelligences because there was more time to do so. It was also clear that on C days teachers condensed the variety of activities to fit the shorter period, planned more cultural activities, or gave tests or quizzes. Additionally, there was evidence that there was more *teacher-directed activity* on C days because less time was available.

## INTERVIEW QUESTIONS (APPENDIX 3.5)

The five questions on this measure all focus on issues of instructional strategies, student learning, and teacher values. Our hope was to see to what degree teacher comments about strategies and values matched what they wrote on their classroom activity logs. In this case, we did interview the same teachers who participated in log activity.

A number of strategies clearly stood out in our conversations with fellow teachers. Both group work and independent student work appear to be strategies that teachers employ readily in the block period. In addition, the interviewees cited the use of demonstrations, by teachers as well as students, as particularly effective within the 100-minute structure. Teachers also noted the effectiveness of class discussions, role-playing games, and simulations. In addition, these educators talked about the ability to explore the use of technology in the classroom while also feeling freer to allow time for students to engage in research during the class period. Finally, many interviewees remarked that given the luxury of time offered by teaching in the block class period, it is possible to devote en-

ergy to encouraging more student presentations and performances.

While these interviews began as conversations about teaching strategies, they quickly turned into discussions around
what we value as educators. In pooling the responses, we first
examined the strategies our peers celebrated, and then we began making connections between them in terms of the values
the various strategies represent. Consider, for example, the issue of using technology as an instructional tool. This idea sur-
faced repeatedly and was repeatedly characterized as an example of teachers valuing *experimentation* and *exploration*, for
themselves as well as for their students. Our conclusion, then,
is that the block period fosters and liberates these values in the
classroom. Shorewood teachers value experimentation and exploration and the challenges that accompany both.

Our interviews also indicate that the same can be said for
*cooperative and collaborative discovery*. Our respondents repeatedly cited the sentiment that the block period allows for
greater flexibility in having students work with each other. In
addition, teachers described their roles as being more collaborative in working with students. In fact, quite a few teachers
suggested that this change in schedule has heralded a change
in the role of teacher, the longer period allowing the professional to present a more personal, more humane manner in the
classroom. For some, this was described as being more realistic
to the world of work.

Further, the teachers interviewed suggested that the classroom in general is becoming more student-directed within the
block-period structure, with greater emphasis being placed on
student independence in an increasingly relaxed learning atmosphere. However, teachers also noted that this trend toward
students assuming greater personal responsibility for their success could result in failure for students unable, for whatever
reasons, to meet this responsibility. For these students, many
teachers feel that more frequent, if not *daily contact* would provide the best type of support.

Finally, the Shorewood teachers participating in the interviews repeatedly echoed the belief that having the time to fo-

cus on a topic is an outcome that the block period allows. Teachers appear to value the chance to pursue an area of study in greater depth than before, simply because they have more focused time at their disposal within a class period.

## STUDENT SURVEY QUESTIONS AND RESULTS (APPENDICES 3.6 AND 3.7)

These data are the most problematic, due in no small part to the fact that they are quite surprising. They are also much less supported than the other data, because there are no interviews to bring explanation and nuance to the numbers presented in Appendix 3.7.

The surprises are many. For example, in a district that to many has been the toast of the state in using technology as a part of instruction, it is discouraging to see students reporting that this is largely not the case, at least in the classes taken by the students sampled (Question 6). At the same time, in an era when so much of assessment is moving toward the assessment of student performances, it is troubling to discover that students are suggesting that they are rarely required to present and exhibit in their classes (Question 3).

Students also note that lecture remains a dominant instructional strategy. Roughly 79% of the respondents report that lecture is a strategy used at least half of the time in classes (Question 2); on the other hand, the student respondents also say that traditional "seat work" consumes roughly half of instructional time (Questions 9 and 12). Little time is devoted to field trips, and few students engage in lab activities in their classes (Questions 14 and 13).

However, working in groups on projects is a common practice; 63% of those surveyed suggest it takes up at least half of instructional time (Question 1). Also, 89% of our students suggest that they are either required or allowed to work with a partner, so the traditional view of the student strapped to a desk while the teacher lectures is tempered by work that takes place in collaboration with peers (Question 9). Also, it must be noted that according to our students, class discussion appears to be a strategy valued in our classrooms; 57% assert that this strategy is used at least half of the time in classes (Question 8).

Taken as a whole, this survey presents a bit of a mixed bag. On the one hand, there are items that surprise and trouble, while there is also evidence that much of what we think is good and useful is actually taking place. However, it is difficult to come to terms with the suggestion that students rarely get the chance to do independent research (Question 4). Once again, it would help to have more detailed and precise data detailing what students mean when they use our terms such as research, multimedia, and worksheets. Student interviews would probably have given us this clarification.

## ACTION PLAN AND CONCLUSION

Our first task is to spend some time in the fall debriefing the findings with the Shorewood faculty. It is obvious that our sense of what happens in the block-period classroom is sometimes quite different from that of our students, and this knowledge must serve as a vehicle to have us reconsider how we are delivering education, as well as how we are being perceived by those who sit in our classrooms. Our findings beg for a greater understanding of the generation gap that appears in the perceptions of the respondents. We believe that it would be fruitful to pursue with our students what their expectations are of quality classroom instruction. More detailed and descriptive data about student attitudes and expectations would enrich our study enormously. As it is, we have only the broad stroke finding that their perceptions are very different from our own. Clearly, it would behoove us to gain greater insight into those differences. We stand to learn much from the feedback we might get from our students. This data might easily be used as a part of an introductory packet for our new teachers, as well as a touchstone for more seasoned educators.

Perhaps one way to gain this deeper understanding would be to create two new instruments to gauge student perceptions. A modified student log, used in concert with the teacher activity log, would help us see where the discrepancies are in our various perceptions. It would also be useful to create a student interview form, much like the one used with teachers. This would be used in conjunction with the teachers' form. In addition to this providing greater depth to our investigations, it would also create a more controlled set of data, as we could be sure that we were actually talking about the same circumstances when we compared data from the different instruments. (Again, one of the problems that we think plagues our data is that we cannot tie student responses to particular teacher comments or logs.)

This study represents a very important chance for our school to reflect on the major initiative of the last 4 years at Shorewood. This work encourages the type of important introspection that we don't always engage in as educators. With the hectic and relentless pace of high school teaching, taking the time to consider research carefully is rarely a priority. Now, with the data from our study, generated by our own colleagues and students, this type of reflection will be more meaningful, more useful, and more necessary.

Finally, one idea for future research has special appeal for the research team. This is the category of *high quality instruction*. What makes a good teacher? What are the qualities of effective teaching, particularly within this new framework of the block period? This investigation would necessarily need to pull from a variety of research alternatives in order to create a picture of effective teaching. For our research team, it grows from a real need to get a clearer sense from students about what they see as being important in the classroom. Their voices are not clear enough in our study, and we need that clarification if we are to be effective partners in the classroom with them.

(Mr. Guthrie and Mr. Hegarty teach English. Mr. Hegarty is also one of the school's librarians. Ms. Louden and Ms. Thom teach Spanish.)

# CRITICAL COMMENTS

Lester Krupp and Ed Bergh, Jr., teachers at Yelm High School in Yelm, Washington wrote most of the following comments. David Marshak added several elements to this commentary.

## THE RESEARCH PROCESS

Shorewood's research process included four distinct parts: a teacher questionnaire, the teaching log, the teacher interviews, and the student survey. Though we commend the researchers for the intent behind each part of the research, we also see some major drawbacks in each part that ultimately render the study's results of little use outside of Shorewood itself. We also recognize, of course, that one of the main purposes for action research is the value of self-study, and we take the researchers' word that this was a highly valuable process for them.

The first problem emerges from the faculty questionnaire. Frankly, we found the questionnaire to be ambiguous. At first, the instruction seems clear: Rate these teaching strategies as more effective in block periods or more effective in 50-minute periods. But the second part of the instruction changes this to "engages a high percentage of students" or "has limited success." Does the question ask about these techniques in the abstract? In block periods? In block periods as compared with traditional periods? To make this point another way, suppose a respondent felt that lecturing was *more* effective in *traditional* (shorter) periods. What response would that person give? Probably a "1," which the Shorewood researchers later interpret to mean that lecturing is an ineffective technique in general. We find the results of the survey, therefore, ambiguous as well. We are not convinced that these results necessarily show "a great deal of teacher satisfaction with the 100-minute block class period." Though we believe that teachers, on the whole, *are* satisfied, the percentages related to effectiveness of teaching strategies are unpersuasive.

A second limitation of this initial survey is in interpreting what it reveals about teachers. Surely, it cannot be taken to reveal actual practice, as the researchers infer in their conclusions. More likely, it reveals teachers' values and assumptions about teaching. As such, this is useful information; it could be used later to compare with teachers' actual practice. We wondered also to what extent teachers' responses might vary according to subject area, class size, amount of teaching experience, grade level, or other factors.

We applaud the Shorewood team's use of the Teaching Activity Log. Here is a means to tangible, quantifiable data, which in turn allows comparisons both to teachers' values and to students' perceptions of classroom activity. We were disappointed that the logs were only maintained for 1 week. Such a short time, we felt, might not give a true overall picture of teaching strategies. We feel 3 or 4 weeks would give a more accurate picture. A film, for example, or a library research project might well consume much of 1 week, but relatively little of the longer segment. We wonder if a longer log was rejected because it made too great a demand on participants' time. We realize that a balance must be struck between what is optimal and what is practical. Nevertheless, we found the teaching log to be the strongest and most interesting part of the research. For example, the documentation showing that teachers commonly used C days for tests clearly persuaded the staff to consider ways to change this unexpected consequence.

A second insight the researchers derived from the logs is that experienced teachers structure a class period using a carefully selected *sequence* of related activities. This strikes us as important information: It suggests an important basis for discussion about effective teaching in block periods, as well as a possible new focus for professional development. The importance of integrating teaching strategies further qualifies the initial teacher survey, in which 10 teaching strategies were considered *in isolation only*.

Perhaps the greatest gain from these teaching logs is that it affords the chance to compare present practice with past practice. To our disappointment, this was not done. Perhaps it would have been possible, using old plan books for example, to assemble data that could be compared to the current teaching logs. This would give solid, not anecdotal information about whether or not teaching practices have changed. We suggest that Shorewood teachers consider doing this research in the future, particularly in cases where a teacher has taught the same course under both systems.

We also liked the plan of combining these logs with interviews of the teachers. Ideally, we would want to add a third component, the teachers' responses on the initial survey, thus allowing a comparison of values and practices. Questions 1, 2, and 4 on the interview (see Appendix 3.4) seemed to us very useful and direct, likely to elicit relevant information about teachers' impressions of their own teaching. Questions 3 and 5, on the other hand, surprised us. Both questions (*How do you believe the extended periods have affected student learning?* and *Comparing the 50- and 100-minute periods, how do you feel about your job as a teacher?*) raised huge new issues removed both from the initial question and the other research. The conversations, we are sure, must have been interesting, but we don't think that these questions by themselves could add much to the research data.

Concerning the student survey (Appendix 3.5), we concurred with the researchers' later realization that terms such as multimedia and worksheet needed more careful explanation. We also agree that far more than 19 students' responses were needed, and that it would have been helpful to link students' responses with teaching logs. We would also like to mention that the responses (numbers 1–5) have a built-in logical problem: The percentages are set so that "hardly ever" (Response 5) should be the student's answer for most of the items. How often does a single type of activity take up more than half of class time over a typical week? In all likelihood, teachers used 8 or more of the 14 activities in an average week. We think the students' responses would have been more useful if they had been asked to state (1) whether an activity was likely to occur *at all* during a typical week, and (2) whether it would likely happen once, two to three times, or more often.

## SHOREWOOD'S ANALYSIS

We would like to offer some comments in response to the "Findings and Analysis" section of the report. In their comments about the teaching logs and the interviews, the researchers begin to use the phrases "student-directed activity" and "teacher-directed activity." We know these to be powerful and value-laden phrases in educational parlance. We are, however, concerned about what specific activities might be included under the appealing label "student-directed." The writers seem to include not only student presentations and student-led activities, but also solitary activities such as silent reading, library research, and "independent student work." This concerns us because we have seen, both in our own school and in ones we have visited, a tendency to fill the block period by allowing, for example, students' class time for homework or excessive time to complete group tasks.

The researchers point to further problems with this dependence on student-directed time. Students who are not academically mature (e.g., at-risk students) seem to have more problems maintaining their grades and their learning than they did in the old system. We are pleased to see that Shorewood's study has afforded expression to those teachers who have doubts about the effectiveness of the longer periods for at least some of their students. This also shows up in teachers' concerns for students' retention of information over a 48-hour interval between class periods. We hope that the staff will stay mindful of these concerns and work towards supporting these academically weaker students.

To our thinking, the biggest and most important conclusion in the Shorewood study is that "the block period fosters and liberates [teachers'] values in the classroom." The analysis cites two specific values as examples: experimentation–exploration and cooperative–collaborative discovery. If true, this would be a powerful point in favor of a block-period structure. We therefore want to examine closely the basis for this claim and compare it with our reading of the data and with our own experience.

Overall, we were unsure throughout the research whether the block period was being compared with the shortened periods on Fridays (C days) or with shortened periods in the previous six-period day. This makes an important difference, because, as the researchers point out, teachers have tended to set C days aside for tests, quizzes, and other "teacher-directed" activities. Comparisons between A/B-day teaching strategies and C-day teaching strategies are bound to reveal merely those evolving choices.

We are also very concerned that the reasoning that leads to these conclusions is not necessarily credible. The report cites teachers' claims in the interviews that they use technology more in block periods. We wondered, by the way, whether this included computers only, or also video, slides, and other forms of technology. The report goes on to assert that teachers do this because they value experimentation and exploration. Finally, the report claims that block periods therefore support and foster important educational values in ways that shorter periods do not. There are three problems with this reasoning.

First, we would like to see more data showing that teachers really use technology, or any other teaching strategy, more in block periods. This would require comparison with teaching logs from the earlier six-period day. We note, by the way, that the only relevant data in the study is from the students, who say (58%) that technology is used "hardly ever." While we do not necessarily believe the students, we do believe that hard data is needed.

Second, even if it were true that technology is used more frequently, it is not obvious why teachers choose to do so. Teachers' values could be one reason, but so could the need to entertain students, especially in overcrowded classes, or the need to justify district expenditures in expensive equipment, or the idea that technology skills sell in the marketplace. Our point is that the jump to values is a questionable one.

Finally, even if we could ascertain that teachers really were able to manifest their values through using technology, we would not know whether they could not also have manifested these values in other ways in shorter periods. In our own teaching, for example, in two different subject areas, we have always felt that we could embody our values in our teaching in shorter as well as longer periods. The claim that block periods greatly advantage the teacher is simply not borne out by the data and argument presented in the report. Because this claim is both pervasive and controversial, we feel strongly that it deserves very careful presentation and scrutiny.

## THE REAL VALUE OF SHOREWOOD'S RESEARCH

Turning now to an overall look at the research project, we feel a mixture of envy and admiration for what the Shorewood research team and faculty have accomplished. We realize that action research has two principal aims: contribution to the knowledge base of the profession, and improvement of teaching and learning at the research site. Our earlier observations relate mainly to the first of those goals. We are, frankly, disappointed not to have learned more from the research that would directly apply to the problems we see in our own school. On the matter of improving education on site, we are certain that Shorewood's research project has contributed immensely to the quality of practice.

Shorewood's research process emphasized self-reflection at several stages: by the researchers themselves, by participating teachers (nearly half of the faculty actively involved), and by the students who completed the survey. The research helped staff members to focus and frame their concerns and then to bring these to a general discussion in ways that likely will lead to modifications and resolutions. We have constantly struggled against the heavy isolation inherent in educational institutions. This research project has accomplished very much simply by bringing teachers together to look at and talk about their values and their work. We long for an opportunity to participate in such a project at our school.

On one point, we believe that the Shorewood researchers have worried needlessly about an apparent finding that is not a finding at all. Their conclusion mentions a troubling generation gap, an apparent discrepancy between what students perceive to occur in classes and what teachers perceive. Although the admittedly scant student data does show those perceptions, there is no comparable data from teachers about what they perceive, nor is there any summary empirical data about what actually happens. Perhaps the researchers considered teachers' responses about what they value (Appendix 3.2), but we feel these should not be compared with students' perceptions of what is.

Our final message, then, is one of congratulations. We recognize the commitment of time and energy put forth by the research team toward the general good of their school. We sincerely hope that they and the staff will continue to work on the issues raised by the research.

## A FEW LAST WORDS

The Shorewood teachers involved in this study were engaged in their second year of block-period teaching. In this second year, they were very much engaged in experimentation about how to teach effectively in 100-minute periods. In making sense of this study and its findings, it is critical to keep in mind the experimental quality of much of what teachers reported.

- Even with the methodological flaws and limitations of the study, as described earlier, the results suggest a clear direction of movement by teachers from a kind of teaching practice aligned with the conventional model of high school, toward some yet-to-be-defined model of practice that includes many of the elements identified in Chapter 1.

- The discrepancy between the teacher data and the student data suggests that teachers are in the process of change and that their own focus, as reported through the study, is on what is new and different in their teaching, not on what is enduring. This hypothesis would explain why the teachers seem to have overreported what is new compared with students' perceptions. The sample size of students is small, and this could also be a part of the problem. Another hypothesis, of course, is that the teacher-respondents told the teacher-researchers, to some distorting extent, what they thought the researchers wanted to hear.

♦ As indicated in their conclusions, these four teacher-researchers learned in a powerful way how important it is for high school teachers to gather data from their own students about the students' qualitative appraisal of their school experience.

## APPENDIX 3.1. EXTENDED PERIOD SCHEDULE SURVEY

Please jot down 2 issues of concern that you have regarding **the extended period schedule**. When writing down your concerns please make certain that they involve teaching and learning, that they are something that you can influence, and that they are 2 issues about which you are deeply concerned.

**Concern #1:**

**Concern #2:**

survey #1  Research team:  Guthrie, Hegarty, Louden, Thom.

## APPENDIX 3.2. TEACHER SURVEY QUESTIONS

TO : Shorewood HS Staff
FR : David Guthrie, Pat Hegarty, Suzanne Louden, Marian Thorn
RE : Action Research on extended periods

At the present time, many schools nationwide are moving towards extended periods of instruction, like our ABC schedule. While there exists data on the scheduling itself, no research has been done on the effect of extended periods.

Shorewood is a member of a team of ten Western Washington high schools working in conjunction with Seattle University to conduct research on the use of extended periods in our own schools and their effect on teachers and students in regard to learning. The schools involved in the research project are: Cedarest, Decatur, Foster, Gig Harbor, Jackson, Lindbergh, Tahoma, Wilson, Woodinville, and Shorewood. The task of each school team is to formulate a question statement, conduct research and then together compile the information and findings to be published for public knowledge.

The question that we at Shorewood formulated with the staff's help and will begin to research is: How have teaching techniques and strategies changed as a result of extended periods, and what does this tell us about teacher values regarding what leads to learning?

In order to begin our research we ask that you rate the following educational activities on a five-point scale, according to their effectiveness for 100 minute periods as compared to 50 minute periods. In other words, a "5" would mean the activity typically engages a high percentage of students while challenging them academically; a "1" would mean the activity normally has limited success at engaging and challenging students. ( We want to emphasize that the research that we do is for the purpose of describing the effects of extended periods and is NOT for evaluating teaching practices. )

| | More effective | | | | Less effective |
|---|---|---|---|---|---|
| Class discussion | 5 | 4 | 3 | 2 | 1 |
| Library time ( research/computer ) | 5 | 4 | 3 | 2 | 1 |
| Lecture | 5 | 4 | 3 | 2 | 1 |
| Partners | 5 | 4 | 3 | 2 | 1 |
| Group work/coop learning | 5 | 4 | 3 | 2 | 1 |
| Independent work/guided practice | 5 | 4 | 3 | 2 | 1 |
| Presentations ( group, individual ) | 5 | 4 | 3 | 2 | 1 |
| Content related games | 5 | 4 | 3 | 2 | 1 |
| Multimedia ( videos, slides ) | 5 | 4 | 3 | 2 | 1 |
| Simulations ( trials, debates ) | 5 | 4 | 3 | 2 | 1 |
| Other _____ | 5 | 4 | 3 | 2 | 1 |
| ( Please identify ) | | | | | |
| Other _____ | 5 | 4 | 3 | 2 | 1 |
| ( Please identify ) | | | | | |

---

YOU ARE INVITED to be a part of this action research project! We are soliciting 20 teacher volunteers to do two tasks which include
1) keeping a teacher log summarizing one class for one week, and
2) a 15-20 minute interview. If you would like to express your concerns and contribute to this extended-period research project, please sign your name below in the space provided and we will contact you shortly! We appreciate your input!

Yes, _____ from the _____
department would like to volunteer.

## APPENDIX 3.3. RATING INSTRUCTIONAL STRATEGIES—RESULTS

"In order to begin our research, we ask that you rate the following educational activities on a five-point scale, according to their effectiveness for 100 minute periods, as compared to 50 minute periods. In otherwords, a "5" would mean the activity typically engages a high percentage of sents while challengingly them academically; a "1" would mean the activity normally has limited success at engaging and challenging students."

|                   | 5  | 4  | 3  | 2 | 1  |   |
|-------------------|----|----|----|---|----|---|
| Class Discussion  | 22 | 56 | 22 | 0 | 0  | % |
| Library time      | 55 | 22 | 17 | 0 | 6  | % |
| Lecture           | 11 | 21 | 50 | 7 | 11 | % |
| Partners          | 44 | 28 | 28 | 0 | 0  | % |
| Group work        | 74 | 15 | 11 | 0 | 0  | % |
| Independent work  | 36 | 28 | 28 | 8 | 0  | % |
| Presentations     | 52 | 22 | 26 | 0 | 0  | % |
| Games             | 41 | 18 | 27 | 9 | 6  | % |
| Multimedia        | 50 | 29 | 17 | 4 | 0  | % |
| Simulations       | 68 | 32 | 0  | 0 | 0  | % |

# APPENDIX 3.4. TEACHING ACTIVITY LOG

Choose one class, and for one week - AAC, or BBC - record the activities that you and the students engage in, marking the amount of time spent on each activity during that period. Please use the category list provided below to ensure a common vocabulary.

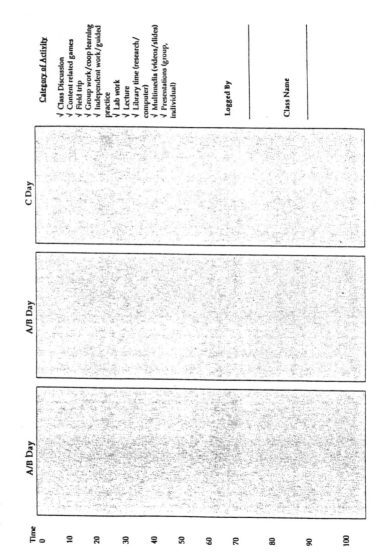

**Category of Activity**

√ Class Discussion
√ Content related games
√ Field trip
√ Group work/coop learning
√ Independent work/guided practice
√ Lab work
√ Lecture
√ Library time (research/computer)
√ Multimedia (videos/slides)
√ Presentations (group, individual)

Logged By _____

Class Name _____

Time: 0, 10, 20, 30, 40, 50, 60, 70, 80, 90, 100

A/B Day      A/B Day      C Day

## APPENDIX 3.5. TEACHER INTERVIEW QUESTIONS

1. What are the instructional strategies that you use most in the extended period?

2. How are you teaching differently from the 50 minute period?

3. How do you believe the extended periods have affected student learning?

4. What are some specific projects or assignments that you have used in extended periods that were not well suited to 50 minute periods?

5. Comparing the 50 and 100 minute periods, how do you feel about your job as a teacher?

## APPENDIX 3.6. STUDENT SURVEY QUESTIONS

Directions:    Mark the response that correctly identifies the percentage of time you spend during *an average week* on the following activities in your **third period class.**

1. Most of the time. (Almost 100% of the time.)
2. Much of the time. (At least 70% of the time.)
3. Half of the time. (At least 50% of the time.)
4. Some of the time. (At least 25%.)
5. Hardly ever. (Less than 25%.)

1. In this class the teacher has me work in small groups with other students to complete an   assignment, plan a presentation, or work on a long term project.

2. In this class the teacher spends time lecturing to the class. (Talking to the class about the subject matter, while students listen and take notes.)

3. In this class the teacher I am required to make presentations and present exhibitions of my work to the rest of the class.

4. In this class I spend time and energy doing independent research in the library, or outside of school.

5. In this class we play games to help us learn the subject matter.

6. In this class the teacher uses multimedia devices (VCR, Slide Projector, Laserdiscs, etc.) to help teach the class.

7. In this class I participate in simulation activities such as debates, plays, role-playing, mock trials, etc.

8. In this class we spend time participating in general class discussions.

9. In this class we are required/allowed to work with a partner.

10. In this class I do seat work consisting of writing assignments, worksheets, etc.

11. In this class I do silent reading at my desk.

12. In this class I do work at my seat while the teacher periodically comes by my desk to check in on how I'm doing. (Guided Practice)

13. In this class we participate in fieldtrips.

14. In this class I do labs.

## APPENDIX 3.7. STUDENT SURVEY RESULTS

Numbers in the lettered columns are percentages of the total group responding.

|     | A | B | C | D | E |
|-----|------|------|------|------|------|
| 1 | 10.5 | 21 | 31.5 | 26.3 | 5.2 |
| 2 | 10.5 | 36.8 | 31.5 | 21 | 0 |
| 3 | 0 | 10.5 | 5.2 | 36.8 | 47.3 |
| 4 | 0 | 10.5 | 5.2 | 21 | 63.1 |
| 5 | 10.5 | 10.5 | 15.7 | 10.5 | 52.6 |
| 6 | 0 | 5.2 | 21 | 15.7 | 57.8 |
| 7 | 5.2 | 15.7 | 10.5 | 15.7 | 52.6 |
| 8 | 15.7 | 31.5 | 10.5 | 21 | 21 |
| 9 | 31.5 | 31.5 | 26.3 | 5.2 | 5.2 |
| 10 | 15.7 | 21 | 15.7 | 26.3 | 21 |
| 11 | 0 | 5.2 | 10.5 | 10.5 | 73.6 |
| 12 | 5.2 | 21 | 15.7 | 15.7 | 42.1 |
| 13 | 0 | 5.2 | 0 | 15.7 | 73.6 |
| 14 | 5.2 | 10.5 | 5.2 | 5.2 | 68.4 |

**4**

# GIG HARBOR HIGH SCHOOL

## A STUDY OF STUDENTS' AND TEACHERS' PERCEPTIONS REGARDING EFFECTIVE LEARNING ACTIVITIES IN BLOCK PERIODS

Ken Brown, Daniel Dizon,
Sherri Patterson, Derek Sheffield

### SCHOOL PORTRAIT AND INTRODUCTION

Gig Harbor High School is in Gig Harbor, Washington, across Puget Sound from the city of Tacoma. It has an enrollment of approximately 1,400 students. About 6 percent of the students are persons of color. Although the city of Gig Harbor is rapidly expanding, it still retains its small town feeling.

Gig Harbor High School was one of the first schools in Washington State to move to a block schedule. Students complete six classes each semester. On "even days," periods 2, 4, and 6 meet. On "odd days," periods 1, 3, and 5 are held. Each class is 100 minutes long and even and odd days always alternate.

An important part of the schedule is a meeting called *Teams*. *Teams* meet on odd days between first and third period. Each teacher, counselor, and principal is in charge of approximately 20 students who compose their *Teams* class. During this half-hour, assemblies are held, scheduling is done, and students may visit their classroom teachers for help or makeups. It is a chance for teachers and students to get to know each other in a nongraded class. On even days, this half-hour is tacked onto second period and is reserved for sustained silent reading. The entire staff, including clerical staff, are expected to read. On Fridays, there is no meeting during this time, and school gets out 30 minutes early. Students may use these 30 minutes after school on Fridays to get extra help in their classes.

The decision to move to a block schedule was not an easy one. Many teachers were very concerned about keeping students actively involved for 100 minutes. In general, the science, physical education, art, English, and social studies faculty were all for it. Math, keyboarding, and foreign language teachers were nervous about the large block of time as well as the absence of daily contact. Before and during the first year of the block schedule, inservice staff development was offered. Strategies for keeping students actively involved were presented on the staff days before the school year started and on half days during the year. The focus was on using cooperative groups and partner work in academic subjects. Many departments also met to discuss what was and wasn't working for them. Keeping the lines of communication open was extremely important.

After 4 years of working with this schedule, all but one member of the faculty is convinced that it really does work best. Each year the staff, students, and parents have evaluated the schedule. The response is undeniably favorable. The workload for students and staff is manageable, and the overall pace of the day is more relaxing. Test scores have continued to rise, and absences have decreased. Gig Harbor's student attendance rate averages 94% to 96% each day throughout the year. When asked, most members of the staff are extremely resistive to going back to a six-period day. If anything, the discussion has been about whether or not the classes should be extended even longer.

## RESEARCH METHODOLOGY

After a series of meetings, the Gig Harbor High School action research team decided to create a research question informed by two questions: What can we reasonably survey given the time frame? Can the research results be useful for us as teachers upon completion?

We began by meeting after school to brainstorm topics we found interesting. We narrowed this list down, and from these topics wrote questions we wanted to answer. Finally, keeping our interests and the school's interests in mind, we decided on a question: *What do students and teachers perceive as the most effective combinations of activities in 100-minute lessons?*

To investigate our question, we decided to create and administer two surveys—one for teachers and a separate one for students. These draft surveys were then brought to select members of our school faculty for comments. Our committee then revised the surveys based on this feedback and developed the final versions, which appear in Appendices 4.1 and 4.2.

Our student survey was designed to answer our research question as well as a simpler question: *What do students and teachers perceive as the most effective instructional strategies in the 100-minute period?* This second question ignored the *combinations* of activities and instead focused just on the activities themselves. On our survey, Questions 1 and 2 were designed to elicit information that we were not certain would prove useful or interesting: grade level and cumulative grade-point average. Question 3 was meant to determine student preferences as to combinations of activities which students felt were most effective in the block period. Question 4 was designed to determine student opinion as to the most effective activities, regardless of combinations, order, or time devoted to these activities. In addition, Question 4 allowed for other activities to be filled in by the respondent, presumably those activities, if any, which were overlooked in our survey's design (see Appendix 4.2).

Our team's teacher survey was designed to be parallel to the student survey. Question 1 was asked, as in the student survey, to elicit information that would perhaps prove interesting, worth discussing, or researching further upon completion of our project. Questions 2 and 4 attempted to investigate teacher beliefs as to the most effective combinations of activities. Question 3 was designed to determine what teachers perceived as effective activities, regardless of order or combination (see Appendix 4.1).

In April 1996, our research team administered the surveys to our faculty and staff. We chose a staff meeting as the forum for the survey and requested all 34 teachers present at that meeting to complete the four-question teacher survey. The 34 teachers included about 60 percent of the faculty and represented all departments. We allowed the staff 15 minutes to finish the survey to encourage well-articulated answers to our questions. Most teachers finished the survey in 5–10 minutes.

Our action research team also administered the student survey in April. We chose several courses that were homogeneous in terms of student grade level. Students in Washington State History (a 9th-grade class), Western Civilization (a 10th-grade class), American Studies (an integrated American literature and United States history course for 11th graders), and American Political Behavior (a 12th-grade course) completed the surveys in class. With the exception of the class of seniors, our team members were the teachers of these classes, and therefore we administered the surveys to our own students. In the case of the senior class, one team member administered the survey to a colleague's class with his permission. In addition, several seniors in one team member's *Teams* advisory class were surveyed. In total, 75 students from each of the four grade levels were surveyed.

Overall, we were satisfied with the survey administration process. Administering the surveys ourselves was a good way to prevent researcher bias from compromising our results. Before administering the surveys, we met and agreed upon a set of simple and clear directions to give our respondent students and staff. This allowed for uniform administration of surveys.

Asking teachers to complete the survey during a staff meeting proved to be a successful method for ensuring all surveys were completed promptly and accurately. The tendency of busy staff members to misplace or forget about surveys was avoided through this method.

## FINDINGS AND ANALYSIS

Perhaps our most profound error in the research process became evident on collection of the surveys and analysis of our data. As discussed later, our surveys seemed to be most effective in addressing our peripheral question regarding what students and teachers perceived as the most successful activities in isolation, regardless of their combination with other activities. In other words, the most interesting results of our surveys were attained through responses to Question 4 of the student survey and Question 3 of the teacher survey (the questions using the objective rating scale as to individual activities' efficacy in the block period). This may be due to the rating scale used in these questions as opposed to the open-ended nature of the others. Compiling the data from the more open-ended questions on the surveys proved difficult due to the wide range of respondent answers. We ended up attempting to find tendencies in responses and grouping like answers together. This compromised the validity of our results to our main research question regarding combinations of activities. The bulk of our findings, then, focus on this second, peripheral research question.

A second error made in the research process related to Question 3 of the teacher survey, and Question 4 of the student survey—the questions offering 10 possible educational activities followed by a 5-point rating scale (see Appendices 4.1 and 4.2). Upon analysis of the data, our team determined that students and teachers might have had different ideas in mind regarding the educational activities when they rated them. The *lecture* activity listed on the survey, for example, may have been interpreted by some respondents to be the traditional teacher-centered oratory, while others may have understood the term *lecture* to mean explanation or setting-up of activities. In this way, different respondents may have rated these activities differently according to individual interpretations of the meaning of the survey's terminology. To avoid this problem, our survey should have explained our terms more precisely by, for example, defining *lecture* as "lecturing of information (not explaining an activity)."

Even with these limitations, we found our data to be interesting and informative, particularly the student responses. The most accurate and reliable data came from responses to Question 4 on the student survey (see Appendix 4.2). Across all grade levels and grade point averages, students rated class discussion, group work, and content-related games as the most effective activities in the 100-minute period. All three of these rated from slightly under to slightly over 4 on a 5-point scale, with a score of 1 meaning not effective and 5 meaning highly effective (see Appendix 4.3). Scoring lowest on the same scale were library time, with a score of under 3, and lecture, with a score of about 3.25.

Student responses to Question 3 on the survey highlighted three combinations of learning activities. Cited most often by students as "interesting and educational" was *lecture followed by group work, lecture, group work, then independent work*, and *lecture followed by group work, then class discussion*. Lecture/group work was cited by students 24 times; lecture/group work/independent work was cited 11 times; and lecture/group work/class discussion 10 times (see Appendix 4.4).

The teachers' responses were generally similar to the students' responses. On Question 3, teachers across disciplines and grade levels taught rated presentations/exhibitions as the most effective for student learning, with an average score of 4.3 on a 5-point scale. Second was simulations, with a score of 4.17. Finally, teachers rated group work as the third best, with a score of 4.12. Rated as least effective by teachers were lecture, with a score of 2.64, and library time, with a score of 2.88 (see Appendix 4.6).

On Question 4 of the survey, which asked for top combinations of activities thought to be "best...for student learning" in the 100-minute period, teachers listed *class discussion, followed by group work and then presentations* the most often. The combination listed the second greatest number of times was *lecture, class discussion, then independent work.* Finally, cited third most often by teachers was *lecture, followed by group work, then independent work* (see Appendix 4.7).

In examining our findings, we were especially intrigued by the results from the question which asked both students and teachers to rate the most effective educational activities from a list of 10 (Questions 4 and 3, respectively; see Appendices 4.2 and 4.1, respectively). This question, we discovered, was the clearest and most relevant one for both groups. Focusing on the top two activities rated by both groups, we noticed that both chose student-centered activities: teachers rated presentations and simulations the highest, while students found discussion and group work to be most effective. We understand that classroom discussion can be more or less student-centered, but given the trends in all of our data we believe students are referring more to the student-centered variety.

The ratings of these active learning strategies by both students and teachers leads us to believe that they are indeed being used at Gig Harbor High in a wide range of subjects. Teachers are using the professional development in alternative teaching methods they received 5 years ago. We also believe that 100-minute periods provide an ideal time frame for such activities, thus encouraging their use. In 100 minutes, for example, teachers are able to explain a project in 15 minutes, give groups 65–75 minutes to accomplish a task, and still have 10–20 minutes for closure. So, as opposed to a 55-minute period schedule, the block-period schedule allows teachers to use what they believe to be more effective learning strategies which require more time, such as simulations and student presentations/exhibitions. Simultaneously, students appreciate being more involved in their own education through active learning activities such as discussion and group work.

Not only do 100-minute periods allow more student-centered teaching, they also seem to force us in that direction. We have come to this conclusion based on the fascinating result that both students and teachers rated library time and lecture as the two least effective educational activities. This finding suggests two conclusions. Teachers are limiting their use of the lecture, while students are still sitting through some lectures and feeling unengaged. In other words, this apparent paradox can be explained by understanding that even though both groups believe the lecture to be ineffective, 4 years into Gig Harbor's block-period schedule teachers are still searching for different ways to communicate information to their students. The schedule is still nudging the teachers away from 55-minute lessons toward the more student-centered variety called for by 100-minute periods.

About library time, we have concluded, from its low rating and our own observations, that students may not have the research skills they need to use the time productively. The facility itself may also be a factor. Gig Harbor High School has a small library with one librarian. There is only one computer with limited access to the Internet, which students can use only with staff assistance. Students may also not have a detailed enough idea of what they need to accomplish during their time in the library.

Library use is one area where we see an obvious change we can make in our own teaching. As part of our action plan, we plan to devote class time to providing our students with more explicit instruction in research methods while making them more directly accountable for their use of research time. This accountability can range from a check-off list students work through as they search different parts of the library to "points" for observed on-task behavior.

Finally, in the first half of their surveys, students and teachers were asked to identify the most effective combinations of learning activities in the classroom (see Appendices 4.1 and 4.2). In examining responses to these questions, we noticed that, even though the lecture had fared poorly in the questions about individual activities, it appeared in the most popular combination of activities cited by both teachers and students (*lecture, class discussion, independent work*). Further, it can be found in the second, third, and fourth choices of both groups.

We believe this finding can be partially explained by the broadness of the term *lecture*, within which respondents must have included the kind of explanatory remarks a teacher would make in setting up a group activity. We believe it also makes sense, however, that lecture would be an important part of successful teaching combinations because it provides variety when used with two very student-centered activities such as group work and class discussion. Thus, both students and teachers appreciate variety in 100-minute periods.

## ACTION PLAN

In addition to the adjustment mentioned in the previous section in our use of library time, we have discussed a desire to make other changes in our teaching. Our results confirmed a suspicion we already held: Lecture is ineffective as the primary educational method in the classroom. Even though we already knew this, it is comforting to have data from our own school in support of this conclusion. However, our results have revealed something new to all of us and that is the importance of lecture-like explanation and set-up so students are clear about their goal in a project or group activity. We intend to spend more time preparing our introductions to student-centered activities by incorporating engaging sets and presenting students with written directions. We decided also that if we have the time, it is helpful to rehearse the directions with another teacher to receive feedback regarding clarity.

We also have been reminded of the importance of variety in 100 minutes. In our planning, we intend to "mix it up," to shift gears from teacher-centered activities to student-centered ones in the same period. Also, we plan to extend the results somewhat to encourage ourselves to employ different kinds of evaluative methods. These can include writing, speeches, visual and poster-like projects, dramatic reenactments, and so on. This is the most significant realization of our research, the key role of variety. And this is the criterion we will use to evaluate our own teaching in the future.

Our research has not led us to another question, but rather it has led us back to our original one. As noted earlier, we have better answered another question, *What are the most effective kinds of activities for student learning being used in extended periods at Gig Harbor High School?*, than the one we set out to explore. With these results, we have learned much about what is happening in classrooms in our school and about what we need to emphasize in our teaching. Given a second opportunity at this action research, we would try to answer our original question more effectively by giving students and teachers a log to chart their time in the classroom throughout 1 week of school or perhaps longer.

(Mr. Brown teaches social studies. Mr. Dizon teaches special education and social studies. Ms. Patterson teaches mathematics. Mr. Sheffield teaches English and American Studies.)

## CRITICAL COMMENTS

Most of the following comments were written by Christie Christman and Ross Moutier, who teach at South Kitsap High School in Port Orchard, Washington. David Marshak added several elements to this commentary.

## THE RESEARCH QUESTION

When we considered the research question asked by Gig Harbor's team, several responses came immediately to mind. First, all of us who want to be good teachers within the block-period schedule need to understand the answers to their question: *What do students and teachers perceive as the most effective combinations of activities in 100-minute lessons?* A serious problem arises immediately, however, as we look closely at the question. What exactly does "effective" mean? For one student it might mean, "You kept me interested," and for another, "I learned a lot." Effective for one teacher might mean, "Under control," while for another it might mean, "The students talked enthusiastically." In addition, the whole area of preferred delivery methods needs to be examined. Some teachers are dynamite speakers—captivating, funny and informative—while others could have the group snoring after the introduction. Students responding to the survey would need to have very specific instructions about the definitions of terms. An effort at clarification was made on the student questionnaire on Question 3 by replacing "effective" with "interesting and educational."

## FINDINGS AND ANALYSIS

The Gig Harbor researchers have recognized the strengths and weaknesses of their study and discussed them thoughtfully. We appreciate the clarity of their scrutiny of their own efforts.

With the best intentions, it seems that the Gig Harbor team has discovered the obvious. Yes, most students and most teachers appreciate variety in their lessons. What does this research information show as being different between a 100-minute period and a 55-minute period? Is the variety of a six-period day the changing of classes and lecturers? Isn't something that would be dull and tedious in 55 minutes just going to be more dull and tedious in 100 minutes? Although the research attempted to show which various groupings of activities were favored by both students and teachers, the structure of the research, unfortunately, did not allow for significant data to be collected. Guided by the term "effective," the survey asked for perceptions. The report fails to contain information about cognitive growth. Where do we find out if students actually learned anything? We only know how they felt about the "effectiveness" of the experience.

The survey's rating scale for perceived effectiveness seems skewed, and the conclusions seem to be reaching. First of all, does 3.25 on a scale of 5 label a teaching strategy as ineffective? In fact, there is a lack of real difference between the high (4.1) and the low (2.9) scores. There is only a deviation of 1.2 points. The chart format that the researchers use to show the differences in numerical rating renders the data easy to read, but the scale doesn't lend itself to easy understanding. Perhaps a 10-

point or even a 100-point scale would give more room for variation, allowing more "wiggle room" to discriminate among the different levels of effectiveness.

One of the key terms, "lecture," seems to be a problem. By the Gig Harbor team's own admission, the term is vague. Are we discussing input in the traditional college format, or are we talking about instructions, demonstrations, examples, or just "teacher talk"? Lecture is deemed ineffective by the team, yet their evidence seems to contradict this assumption. Lecture scored 3.26 of a possible 5 on the student rating (though only 2.64 on the teacher rating). Lecture is included in all three of the effective lesson plans in the student survey. In addition, it is mentioned in two of the three plans cited by teachers. Does this imply that lecture by itself is ineffective, but it becomes more valuable in combination with other modes of learning?

In our analysis of the results of the survey, we found that teachers highly rated a more formal, product-driven lesson, such as presentation/exhibition and simulation. In contrast, students seemed to prefer less formal, process-driven approaches such as group work and class discussions. The researchers called the survey results "generally similar." Are they? Are teachers and students just using different terms for the same lesson design, or are these truly different activities? We do not see the activities as parallel, but as product-driven versus process-driven. We see that the teachers seemed to value a more formal lesson plan while the students preferred a more informal one. The need for accountability in the learning process is noted in the teachers' top three choices. Product-driven performances, which could be used to assess student achievement, seem key to effectiveness for the teachers. This connection between accountability and effectiveness is unexplored by the researchers and perhaps could lead to additional research.

## THREE KEY ISSUES

The Gig Harbor High School study highlights three interesting and significant issues in relation to block periods.

- The majority of students and teachers who provided data to this study convey their beliefs that learning activities that feature active roles for students are more "effective...for student learning" than activities that tend toward passive roles. It seems reasonable to conclude that experience in block periods during the past 4 years has helped to generate these beliefs.

- The one anomalous finding has to do with the uses of library time. The teacher-researchers hypothesize that this seemingly active, student-centered activity has received a relatively low rating because many students lack the skills to use this time effectively. This finding and hypothesis support the notion that as teachers invite students to become more responsible for their own learning, teachers have an obligation to help students develop the awareness and skills required to enact these responsibilities effectively.

- This study raises the issue of how to structure combinations of learning activities effectively in block periods. Given the methodological limitations of this study, the only supported finding in relation to this question is that most teachers and students believe that variety in learning activities is required for effective use of block periods. Clearly, this is an important insight if an obvious one, given common sense analysis of the issue. And just as clearly, the question about how to structure combinations of teaching and learning activities, largely unanswered by the Gig Harbor study, begs further research.

## OUR CONCLUSIONS

We applaud the attempt of Gig Harbor High School's action research team to come to grips with a very important and complex question. We feel that they have uncovered the tip of the iceberg. Their research seems to have identified the need for further study, rather than being conclusive in and of itself.

## FUTURE RESEARCH IDEAS

Possible future research could investigate the value of individual processing during any learning activity, the old 10–2 rule; that is, 10 minutes of input and 2 minutes of processing to help a learner assimilate new information may make all the difference between what is "covered" and what is "learned." Where is the hard data that could prove this truism? Could the effectiveness of even "lecture" be improved by such attention to individual processing? For example, the tried and true method of note-taking for lecture, reading, films, or other methods of input might not be the most entertaining way of getting and keeping information, but it might be a way of engaging the learner's mind. Classifying lecture as "ineffective" is an example of the inconclusive and subjective nature of Gig Harbor's investigation.

We would like to see this, the research team's idea of a log to chart time usage, further developed. How would the log be used? What would be the usefulness of the information gathered? Would a record be kept of the number of minutes devoted to certain instructional strategies and then the effectiveness of these strategies be tested both by the perception of learning and objective mastery of skills and content? If so, then the log idea would be great! If nothing more were done with it, it would be a waste of time.

A weakness in Gig Harbor's design seems to be that we were given information about how students perceived the effectiveness of their instruction, but nothing at all about what they learned. What would happen if the format of the research were changed such that one teacher delivered the same information to different groups using the three favored teaching outlines from the Gig Harbor research and then tested the students in two ways? For example, a teacher having three sophomore English classes might deliver information to period 1 using the most popular lesson outline of class discussion followed by group work and then presentations. Period 2 could get the same input using lecture, group discussion, and then independent work, which was cited as the second most effective combination. Period 3 could receive the same information using lecture followed by group work and then independent work, cited third most effective in the survey. Then the students would need to be tested. First, it would be vital to discover if students learned and retained content and skills. Second, we would need to know how students felt about what they learned and how they learned it.

Perhaps a way to build in further objectivity and less reliance upon perception would be to use an auditor to observe the target lesson. The auditor would take anecdotal records of the lesson. Perhaps the auditor could additionally chart student on-task behavior. This logging would be followed up by surveys of the teacher and students regarding effectiveness and would need to include some objective measure of student achievement. The auditor's survey could evaluate effectiveness based upon preestablished standards. The three surveys could be compared, providing more of a basis for reliability.

## APPENDIX 4.1. TEACHER SURVEY

1. Please list subjects and grade levels you teach:

2. (a) Choose one 100 minute lesson that you thought was especially effective for student learning. Describe the lesson by providing a sequential list of the activities (ie. lecture, group project, etc.) along with the amount of time spent on each.

2. (b) How did you know this lesson was particularly effective for student learning?

3. Rate the following educational activities according to their overall effectiveness for student learning by circling a number for each activity. In other words, a "5" would mean the activity typically engages a high percentage of students while challenging them academically; a "1" would mean the activity normally has limited success at engaging and challenging students.

| | Most effective | | | | Least effective |
|---|---|---|---|---|---|
| class discussion | 5 | 4 | 3 | 2 | 1 |
| library time (research/computer) | 5 | 4 | 3 | 2 | 1 |
| lecture | 5 | 4 | 3 | 2 | 1 |
| partners/peer editing | 5 | 4 | 3 | 2 | 1 |
| group work/cooperative learning | 5 | 4 | 3 | 2 | 1 |
| independent work (not homework) | 5 | 4 | 3 | 2 | 1 |
| presentations/exhibitions | 5 | 4 | 3 | 2 | 1 |
| content related games (puzzles, etc.) | 5 | 4 | 3 | 2 | 1 |
| multimedia (video, slides) | 5 | 4 | 3 | 2 | 1 |
| simulations (trials, debates) | 5 | 4 | 3 | 2 | 1 |
| other _____ (please identify) | 5 | 4 | 3 | 2 | 1 |
| other _____ (please identify) | 5 | 4 | 3 | 2 | 1 |
| other _____ (please identify) | 5 | 4 | 3 | 2 | 1 |

4. Choose the three best combinations of these activities for student learning and list them here, along with approximate time spent on each:
(example: lecture--first 20 min., group work--next 40 min., presentation--last 40 min.)

## APPENDIX 4.2. STUDENT SURVEY

1. Grade level (please circle one):     9      10     11     12

2. Cumulative grade point average:   1.0     1.5     2.0     2.5     3.0     3.5     4.0
   (circle closest)

3. Other than P.E., music, and art, choose a class lesson in recent memory that you feel was very interesting and educational. Describe this lesson by discussing the following:

   a) the different activities the teacher used (activities such as lecture, group work, etc.)

   b) in what order they appeared

   c) approximately how much time was spent on each activity

d) what made these activities interesting and educational

4. Rate these educational activities according to their overall effectiveness for student learning by circling one number for each activity. In other words, a "5" would mean that activity kept your attention and you learned a lot from it; a "1" would mean the activity did not keep your attention and you did not learn very much from it.

|  | Most effective | | | | Least effective |
|---|---|---|---|---|---|
| class discussion | 5 | 4 | 3 | 2 | 1 |
| library time (research/computer) | 5 | 4 | 3 | 2 | 1 |
| lecture | 5 | 4 | 3 | 2 | 1 |
| partners/peer editing | 5 | 4 | 3 | 2 | 1 |
| group work/cooperative learning | 5 | 4 | 3 | 2 | 1 |
| independent work (not homework) | 5 | 4 | 3 | 2 | 1 |
| presentations/exhibitions | 5 | 4 | 3 | 2 | 1 |
| content related games (puzzles, etc.) | 5 | 4 | 3 | 2 | 1 |
| multimedia (video, slides) | 5 | 4 | 3 | 2 | 1 |
| simulations (trials, debates) | 5 | 4 | 3 | 2 | 1 |
| other _____ (please identify) | 5 | 4 | 3 | 2 | 1 |
| other _____ (please identify) | 5 | 4 | 3 | 2 | 1 |
| other _____ (please identify) | 5 | 4 | 3 | 2 | 1 |

# APPENDIX 4.3. STUDENT SURVEY DATA: QUESTION 4

## 9th Graders

| | Class Discussion | Simulations | Multimedia | Content Games | Presentations | Indep. Work | Group Work | Partners | Lecture | Library Time | Average |
|---|---|---|---|---|---|---|---|---|---|---|---|
| 4 | 3.5 | 4.69 | 3.93 | 4.14 | 4.43 | 4 | 4 | 3.64 | 3 | 3.36 | 3.87 |
| 3.5 | 3.9 | 4.23 | 4.1 | 3.76 | 3.3 | 3.43 | 4.24 | 4.1 | 2.33 | 2.86 | 3.63 |
| 3 | 3.82 | 3.67 | 4.17 | 4.42 | 3 | 3.83 | 4.75 | 4.42 | 2.64 | 3.08 | 3.78 |
| 2.5 | 3.75 | 4 | 4.57 | 3.71 | 2.88 | 3 | 3.63 | 2.88 | 2.5 | 3.25 | 3.42 |
| 2 | 3.25 | 3 | 3.33 | 3 | 3.5 | 4 | 5 | 4.25 | 2.67 | 3 | 3.50 |
| 1.5 | 3.67 | 3.33 | 3.67 | 4.3 | 2.67 | 3 | 3 | 3 | 2.33 | 2.67 | 3.16 |
| 1 | 5 | 4 | 3 | 3 | 5 | 5 | 5 | 5 | 3 | 4 | 4.10 |
| Average | 3.84 | 3.85 | 3.82 | 3.76 | 3.54 | 3.61 | 4.23 | 3.90 | 2.64 | 3.17 | 3.64 |

## 10th Graders

| | Class Discussion | Simulations | Multimedia | Content Games | Presentations | Indep. Work | Group Work | Partners | Lecture | Library Time | Average |
|---|---|---|---|---|---|---|---|---|---|---|---|
| 4 | 3.9 | 3.67 | 4.14 | 4.13 | 3.73 | 4 | 4.07 | 3.07 | 3.67 | 3.07 | 3.75 |
| 3.5 | 4.36 | 4.09 | 4.35 | 3.96 | 3.81 | 3.75 | 3.86 | 3.14 | 3.18 | 3.24 | 3.77 |
| 3 | 3.87 | 3.81 | 3.9 | 3.95 | 3.59 | 3.8 | 4.5 | 3.63 | 3.33 | 3.41 | 3.78 |
| 2.5 | 3.75 | 3 | 3.62 | 4.17 | 3.62 | 3.62 | 4 | 3.83 | 3.3 | 2.6 | 3.55 |
| 2 | 4.13 | 4.17 | 3.83 | 4.67 | 4.67 | 3.83 | 4.67 | 3.5 | 3 | 2.6 | 3.91 |
| 1.5 | 4 | | | | | | | | | | |
| 1 | | | | | | | | | | | |
| Average | 4.00 | 3.75 | 3.97 | 4.18 | 3.88 | 3.80 | 4.22 | 3.43 | 3.30 | 2.98 | 3.75 |

## 11th Graders

| | Class Discussion | Simulations | Multimedia | Content Games | Presentations | Indep. Work | Group Work | Partners | Lecture | Library Time | Average |
|---|---|---|---|---|---|---|---|---|---|---|---|
| 4 | 4.41 | 3.88 | 3.94 | 3.4 | 3.79 | 4.18 | 3.63 | 3.44 | 3.94 | 3.56 | 3.82 |
| 3.5 | 4.36 | 4.31 | 3.79 | 3.64 | 3.86 | 3.86 | 4.27 | 3.57 | 3.93 | 2.5 | 3.81 |
| 3 | 4.47 | 4.07 | 4.2 | 3.73 | 3.8 | 3.73 | 3.86 | 3.87 | 3.6 | 3.29 | 3.86 |
| 2.5 | 4 | 4.22 | 4.1 | 4.56 | 4.2 | 3.8 | 4.2 | 3.78 | 3.8 | 2.89 | 3.96 |
| 2 | 4.43 | 3.43 | 4.29 | 4 | 3.29 | 3.43 | 3.43 | 3.14 | 3.86 | 2.57 | 3.59 |
| 1.5 | | | | | | | | | | | |
| 1 | | | | | | | | | | | |
| Average | 4.33 | 3.98 | 4.06 | 3.87 | 3.79 | 3.80 | 3.88 | 3.56 | 3.83 | 2.96 | 3.81 |

## 12th Graders

| | Class Discussion | Simulations | Multimedia | Content Games | Presentations | Indep. Work | Group Work | Partners | Lecture | Library Time | Average |
|---|---|---|---|---|---|---|---|---|---|---|---|
| 4 | 4.25 | 3.91 | 3.73 | 3.83 | 3.54 | 4.15 | 3.85 | 3.38 | 3.43 | 2.69 | 3.68 |
| 3.5 | 4.26 | 4.3 | 4.11 | 4 | 3.53 | 3.48 | 4.47 | 3.9 | 3.47 | 3 | 3.85 |
| 3 | 4.31 | 4.6 | 3.38 | 4.07 | 4.15 | 3.55 | 4.23 | 3.62 | 2.69 | 2.92 | 3.75 |
| 2.5 | 3.5 | 3.75 | 3.75 | 3.75 | 2.5 | 4.5 | 3.75 | 3.67 | 2.75 | 3 | 3.49 |
| 2 | 5 | 4 | 3 | 5 | 5 | 1 | 3 | 2 | 4 | 1 | 3.30 |
| 1.5 | | | | | | | | | | | |
| 1 | | | | | | | | | | | |
| Average | 4.26 | 4.11 | 3.59 | 4.13 | 3.74 | 3.34 | 3.86 | 3.31 | 3.27 | 2.52 | 3.61 |

## School Average

| | Class Discussion | Simulations | Multimedia | Content Games | Presentations | Indep. Work | Group Work | Partners | Lecture | Library Time | Average |
|---|---|---|---|---|---|---|---|---|---|---|---|
| 4 | 4.02 | 4.04 | 3.94 | 3.88 | 3.87 | 4.08 | 3.89 | 3.38 | 3.51 | 3.17 | 3.78 |
| 3.5 | 4.22 | 4.23 | 4.09 | 3.84 | 3.63 | 3.63 | 4.21 | 3.68 | 3.23 | 2.90 | 3.77 |
| 3 | 4.12 | 4.04 | 3.91 | 4.04 | 3.64 | 3.73 | 4.34 | 3.89 | 3.07 | 3.18 | 3.79 |
| 2.5 | 3.75 | 3.74 | 4.01 | 4.05 | 3.30 | 3.73 | 3.90 | 3.54 | 3.09 | 2.94 | 3.60 |
| 2 | 4.20 | 3.65 | 3.61 | 4.17 | 4.12 | 3.07 | 4.03 | 3.22 | 3.38 | 2.29 | 3.57 |
| 1.5 | 3.84 | 3.33 | 3.67 | 4.30 | 2.67 | 3.00 | 3.00 | 3.00 | 2.33 | 2.67 | 3.16 |
| 1 | 5.00 | 4.00 | 3.00 | 3.00 | 5.00 | 4.00 | 5.00 | 5.00 | 3.00 | 4.00 | 4.10 |
| Average | 4.11 | 3.92 | 3.86 | 3.98 | 3.74 | 3.64 | 4.05 | 3.55 | 3.26 | 2.91 | 3.70 |

## School Averages, Across Grade Level and GPA

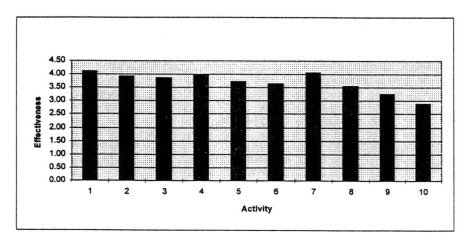

1: Class Discussion
2. Simulations
3. Multimedia
4. Content-Related Games
5. Presentations
6. Independent Work
7. Group Work
8. Partners
9. Lecture
10. Library Time

## APPENDIX 4.4. STUDENT SURVEY DATA: QUESTION 3

# Top 10 Combinations of
# Activities (number of times cited)

Lecture, Group work (24)

Lecture, Group work, Independent work (11)

Lecture, Group work, Class discussion (10)

Lecture, Independent work (10)

Lecture, Class Discussion (8)

Class discussion, Group work (7)

Lecture, Class discussion, Multimedia (6)

Lecture, Group work, Multimedia (4)

Group work, Presentations (4)

Group work, Multimedia (4)

---

**APPENDIX 4.5. TEACHER SURVEY DATA: QUESTION 2(A)**

---

# Three Most Common Lesson Formats

- Warm up/opening activity
- Instruction/lecture
- Group or partner work
- Presentations

- Lecture/set up instructions
- Group work
- Reports/presentations
- Give/start homework assignment

- Lecture/instruction/guided practice
- Labs/activities with groups or partners
- Class discussion
- Handout/homework assignment

## APPENDIX 4.6. TEACHER SURVEY DATA: QUESTION 3

| Activity | Average Rating ( Five-Point Scale ) |
|---|---|
| Class Discussion | 3.72 |
| Simulations | 4.17 |
| Multimedia | 3.52 |
| Content-Related Games | 3.83 |
| Presentations/Exhibitions | 4.30 |
| Independent Work | 3.92 |
| Group Work | 4.12 |
| Partners/Peer Editing | 3.68 |
| Lecture | 2.64 |
| Library Time | 2.88 |

---

**APPENDIX 4.7. TEACHER SURVEY DATA: QUESTION 4**

---

# Most Popular Combinations of Activities

- Class discussion
- Group work/cooperative learning
- Presentations

- Lecture
- Class Discussion
- Independent Work

- Lecture
- Group Work
- Independent Work

- Lecture
- Group Work
- Independent Work

- Lecture
- Group Work
- Presentations

- Multimedia
- Lecture
- Group Work

# 5

# CEDARCREST HIGH SCHOOL
## THE EFFECTIVENESS OF LEARNING ACTIVITIES AND THE USE OF TIME IN THE BLOCK PERIOD

Feather Alexander, Mark Lovre
Allen Olson, Anthony L. Smith

## SCHOOL PORTRAIT AND INTRODUCTION

Cedarcrest High School is a 4-year school located in Duvall, Washington, the only high school in the Riverview School District in east King County, about 25 miles east of Seattle. Cedarcrest serves more than 700 students in the rapidly growing lower Snoqualmie River Valley, a rural and exurban area that includes three small towns. About 10 percent of the students are persons of color.

Cedarcrest High School opened in 1993, replacing predecessor grades 7 through 12 school, with a reform-based structure called the Cedarcrest Plan.

The core elements of the Plan include:

- A daily schedule that requires students to take only three classes per 9-week term. With 100-minute classes, a semester's work is completed in 9 weeks, and teachers are able to develop lessons in greater depth, focus on students as individuals, and build stronger relationships with students.

- A 37-minute daily advisory period which gives all students the opportunity to have study time daily, have a student advocate who will be assigned to them for 4 years, and improve the communication network with home. In addition, advisory class is an opportunity for every student to have daily contact with a teacher throughout the student's high school career.

- A required student portfolio that is in advance of recent state legislation to mandate this element for all high school graduates, enables the student to collect an exhibition of written and nonwritten work.

- A required senior project with three main elements: paper, project, and presentation.

- A social skills plan that addresses student needs to exhibit desirable personal qualities that society expects from a high school graduate, and a student recognition program that recognizes the positive contributions of Cedarcrest students.

The three-period day has been in place at Cedarcrest for 3 years. There are a variety of advantages and disadvantages depending on which staff member, student, parent, or community member is interviewed. Listed here are the relative strengths and weaknesses of the Cedarcrest Plan as perceived by the research team.

## STRENGTHS

Extended blocks of time for each class period
Advisory program

Ability to rapidly advance through course sequences

Teachers work with fewer students per term.

More contact time for teachers with students

Less fragmentation (in terms of number of classes, passing time, student and teacher workload, etc.)

Club and activity meetings during advisory period

Fewer class interruptions

### WEAKNESSES

Extended blocks are difficult for some students

Advisory program lacks organization

Music program has suffered because students cannot afford to take it year-round

No yearlong courses are offered

Limitations in course sequencing

Limitations in the flexibility of the master schedule

Absences by students are much harder to make up

Homework load can easily become unbalanced (two or three easy classes one term, three hard classes the next)

Teachers only have planning time for half of the year

Currently, Cedarcrest is again in the restructuring process, exploring the faculty's issues and concerns with the current structure. Planning time is a concern, because teachers have 100 minutes of planning time each day for one semester and no planning time at all the other semester. The faculty and administration are working on adding or reshaping elements that need improvement while keeping the integrity of the advantages of the Cedarcrest Plan. Thoughts range from splitting a block, to creating some yearlong offerings, to looking at other scheduling models.

From the students' perspectives, the school's structure seems to be working well. During the interviews conducted for this research project, many students commented on the block periods. Most of the comments were positive and should help allay the fears of anyone who thinks that students cannot handle longer periods. A group of freshmen commented that they were adjusted to the 100-minute periods. "It makes the day go by faster," one student claimed. "I learn more," said another. They liked the fact that a teacher could assign longer assignments and that they would have more time to complete them. A senior who had experienced the traditional six-period day during her freshman year pointed out some of the drawbacks of the block periods. She still felt there was too much lecturing and that she had more total homework each night than she had had in the six-period day. One other criticism of the Cedarcrest Plan concerned the fact that a year in the old system was now taught in a semester. As she put it, teachers must "cram the stuff you're doing in 1 year into half a year, so you have half as many nights to think about it." This issue was also raised by teachers and the staff in their discussions of the advantages and disadvantages of the school's structure.

## RESEARCH METHODOLOGY

As a team of teachers in a block-period schedule, we wanted our research to focus on an issue in which we were active participants, one which directly affected us and which would help us and our colleagues become more reflective about our practice, finding new ways to grow professionally as a result of this study. Thus, we used a collaborative action research approach to study the 100-minute period at our own Cedarcrest High School, understand what is happening in the classrooms, and discover new and better methods of practice.

Issues of time use seemed to be the most common concerns raised in our initial discussions of the effectiveness of block periods. We wondered how the longer block of time was used. We had been told that one of the major advantages of block periods was that they forced teachers to be more creative in their use of time. Lecturing for 80, 90, or 100 minutes is not an option. We wondered what was actually happening during those 100 minutes. What routines do teachers use? What types of activities are used? How are monotony and boredom avoided? Is the time just "given up" to let students work on homework? Does using a variety of activities affect how deep or how broad the lessons are?

We soon realized that we could not answer all of these questions and that the answers might be different for each subject, if not for every teacher. We decided to take a step back and let the teachers, students, and administrators advise us on the effectiveness of different activities. To take full advantage of this variety of resources, we settled on the following central research question: *How does one structure time for effective teaching and learning in a block period?*

There are two major issues involved in this question. The first is the pervasive issue of time. The second is the issue of effective teaching and learning. We immediately realized that we had no clear definition of "effective," and therefore had no way of measuring the effectiveness of any particular structure in terms of teaching or learning. Instead of attempting to find a single, comprehensive measure of effectiveness, we decided to focus on finding a working definition of "effective" as it applies to teaching and learning in block periods. Therefore, we broke our overall research question down into these subquestions:

- How much time is spent in each type of activity in the classroom?
- How is effective teaching defined?

These questions clearly reflect the two major issues of the central research question, and they can be approached separately using different research methods. The first question was initially researched through surveys. The second question was approached through interviews.

To find out how much time is spent in different types of activities, we decided to rely primarily on the reports of teachers. We conducted a teacher survey in two steps. First, we used 15 minutes of a faculty meeting to brainstorm classroom activities that teachers use at Cedarcrest High School. We described our research project to the teachers and gave them a sheet of paper with instructions to "list all instructional techniques and activities that occur in your classroom" (see Appendix 5.1). This sheet also gave teachers an opportunity to provide comments on our study; we asked for suggestions about what our research team should be researching.

After compiling, sorting, and discussing the list of activities, we developed a simple form for teachers to record the activities they used in one class during 1 week. The form (see Appendix 5.2) provided 20-minute time blocks for one period for each day of the week. We distributed this form to teachers and asked them to fill it out as a journal or diary. We hoped to receive records of what actually happened in the classes, not just what the teachers had planned for the week.

The results of this second step in the survey process were unfortunate, yet not surprising. There were many teachers who did not return their survey forms. We did receive completed forms from 12 teachers, about one-third of our faculty, who each had charted one class for a week.

While our data do not include the entire faculty, they do provide a portrait of the teaching of a significant minority of our staff (see Appendix 5.3). As noted in the next section, there are several interesting aspects of the data.

To get more information about the activities themselves and how different activities are used, we then interviewed teachers, students, and administrators. We settled on six interview questions that were adjusted slightly for each group of interviews (see Appendix 5.4). The focus of the questions can be obtained from the questions asked of students:

1. What classroom activities do you enjoy? Why?

2. What classroom activities do you find effective? How do you know they are effective?

3. How much effort do you have to put into these activities? What kind of effort? How does the effort involved relate to your feelings about the activity?

4. What reasons does the teacher give for doing these activities? Why do you think the teacher is having you do these activities?

5. How often are these activities used? Do you think they should be used more or less?

6. How do you define effective teaching in a 100-minute period?

The questions were initially asked of two groups of students. We then selected students randomly until we had a male and female representative from each class. These representatives, 12 students in total, were interviewed individually. All four administrative staff members at the school were interviewed, and eight teachers were selected for interviews through a process of random selection that insured that each department would be represented. The data gathered from all the surveys and interviews were then compiled and sorted to gather the emergent themes and implications.

## FINDINGS AND ANALYSIS

### USE OF CLASS TIME

First of all, it is clear from the completed forms that we received from teachers that the majority of class time is not spent in large group or teacher-centered activities. In all the classes we surveyed, the majority of the time was spent in activities for small groups or individual practice, if doing homework and in-class reading are considered individual practice. According to our data, large-group direct-instruction only takes up about 10% of class time. This confirms our suspicions about one impact of block periods: Teachers do have to structure their time creatively. *Our data clearly indicate that teachers use a variety of activities during the block period.* But because of the simple numerical form of our data, we cannot answer questions about how different activities are used or about the order in which activities are used. We also cannot conclude whether each of the activities was successfully incorporated into each of the lessons. All we can do is report that most of the class time was spent in student-centered activities rather than teacher-centered activities.

## STUDENT INVOLVEMENT AND ENJOYMENT

According to our interviews, the key to enjoyment for students is their level of involvement in an activity. From the perspective of the teacher, the more the students are involved in an activity, the more worthwhile the activity seems to be. The viewpoint of the students is slightly more self-centered, but the students still expressed preferences that made it clear that they wanted to be "doing" something, even if that "doing" was just listening to something interesting or watching an interesting video. One student pointed out that the block periods allowed more activities that involved motion and movement. Getting up and going outside or just into the hall helped keep students involved.

The principal of Cedarcrest made the issue of involvement very explicit. He said that the activities he most enjoyed seeing were ones where "kids are involved in activities that are centered around them." He added that activities where students are actively involved promote their learning in that lesson. The role of the teacher in such activities is to "sit back and act as a facilitator." He even specified a goal for the ratio between teacher-centered and student-centered learning. He would like to see 25% of class time spent on teacher-centered activities and 75% spent on student-centered activities. When asked about the current ratio in the school, he put it at 50–50 and claimed it was going in the right direction.

Two common activities at Cedarcrest that involve students and that many students enjoy, or at least appreciate, are small-group work (25% of the time in our data) and individual practice (28% of the time). In our interviews, group work was praised for both its academic and social value. Most students liked using their hands and having to think, and they also liked the more relaxed atmosphere where they could talk to their friends and still get work done. Yet, student opinions were still diverse. Where one student said, "I remember it better" and "I don't like to be left alone," another said, "It's only dumb people who like to work in groups."

The use of individual practice was clearly important to both students and teachers. Students commented that this allows them more freedom and gives them time to get help. Many students noted that it was nice to have more time to work on projects or to get started on homework so they could get their questions answered. "I hate getting home," one student said, "and not knowing how to do it." By having some time to practice in class, this student felt she could get most of her questions answered so she would know how to do the work when she got home.

Other activities that are often used by teachers in block periods were brought up in several of the interviews. Watching movies and doing "book work" and worksheets were mentioned with mixed opinions. Some students saw such activities as good breaks in the routine that didn't require much effort but could be useful for learning. Other students showed definite preferences for group work and more "hands-on" activities.

The only type of activity that did not continually bring up mixed opinions from the students was discussion. The students enjoyed discussions and felt that they were not used enough in their classes. These students clearly liked the idea of being able to express their opinions and interact with other students in the class rather than just the teacher. Teachers also mentioned discussions as positive experiences. One teacher suggested that open-ended discussion on specific topics or hypothetical questions help keep students interested and make them think. She stated, "Both discussion and brainstorming activities allow students to express their ideas. It also allows me to hear what they think. These activities help to start them thinking about things that could impact their lives and futures." Another teacher liked discussions because they put students on the spot and helped them learn some of the skills of give and take.

## EFFECTIVENESS OF ACTIVITIES

Differences of students' beliefs about the effectiveness of various activities appeared in student responses to our second interview question. When asked which activities were effective, students immediately replied, "None of them!" This was immediately followed by "All of them!" One student felt that activities where she worked alone were the most effective, whereas another felt it was best to work with others. They eventually compromised and decided that "small discussions of problems with your neighbors is best."

Most students seemed to think that group work was the most effective type of activity. Their reasons again ranged from social to academic, but the clear message was that they would get things done and remember what they did as long as they were involved in the work the group was doing. "Getting stuff done" was the key. Group work and individual practice time were consistently praised for the time they provided to work on whatever was necessary. One student even praised discussion because it was time when you could work on other stuff and still listen to the discussion.

In addition to "getting stuff done," other criteria for effective activities were mentioned by students. One said, "I know when I understand things and when I don't understand things." She apparently took it as obvious that understanding was the goal of an effective activity. Other students mentioned understanding explicitly. This idea is closely related to the plea from one student. "Don't lose me," she said in reference to lectures and videos. She felt that both lectures and videos could be effective if they were done right; but the longer they were, the less effective they were. Both students and teachers commented that the same activities could be effective or ineffective depending on how they were used. As one teacher put it. "Any [activities], if prepared well, are effective. All activities become ineffective when overused, including cooperative learning....Variety is important."

One other key point concerning effectiveness came from a group of students who commented that the overall goal of learning something was sometimes achieved more easily if activities were stretched over a few days. They liked to hear it, do it, do homework on it, review it, and then ask questions about the aspects they still didn't know or understand. This insight seems especially important for teachers in block periods because it is often tempting to use one block period for the introduction, practice, and review of a lesson. The students' comments warn against this practice. Overlapping lessons that continue for two periods or longer may be more effective.

From the standpoint of both teachers and administrators, the effectiveness of an activity is often measured in the results, both during and after the activity. Perhaps the principal expressed it best when he stated that there were both tangible and intangible measures of effectiveness. On the one hand, test scores and other assessment results (he especially emphasized exhibitions and performance assessment) provide a good measure of the learning that has happened. However, there are also clues such as the enthusiasm of the students during the activity and how much the students talk about the activity later in the day. From an administrator's standpoint, the effectiveness of some activities could be measured by hearing the students talking about them in the halls with their friends.

One reservation expressed by the principal on the issue of effectiveness concerned the balance between "learning by doing" and rote learning and knowledge of facts. He was clearly taken by the enthusiasm of students who were involved in hands-on activities, but he felt that the pendulum might have swung too far to one side. He acknowledged that there was much information that students just have to know and that drill of these "facts" was being pushed out of the curriculum. He emphasized that there were still good, fun ways to involve students in drill activities through games and competitions. The principal admitted that such activities usually required extra effort and preparation from the teacher, but he felt it was necessary to make sure that certain facts were covered effectively. Interestingly, one group of students also mentioned that games allowed a chance for "fun learning." They claimed that games "get us enthusiastic and motivated about the subject."

Thus, for many of the participants, a definite link exists between activities that are effective and ones that are "fun" or enjoyable.

## EFFORT

The questions about effort evoked interesting responses from both students and teachers. Most students at first felt that most activities did not require much effort. They eventually found that there were definitely some activities that required more effort than others, but they could not find any concrete relationship between the effort required and the effectiveness of the activity. As one student said, "Effort is like a peanut butter sandwich in a pizza restaurant—it doesn't really relate." However, the students did mention that if they put effort into an activity, they usually learned something and they usually felt good about it. They also commented that if something requires a lot of effort and is really stressful, it takes the fun out of it. They were especially disappointed when they put a lot of effort into activities and then did not get a good grade.

From the teachers' standpoint, effort is necessary to make an activity work. One teacher said she has to put a lot of energy and effort into things because she expects that of her students. This idea was repeated by the principal who said, "If students see teacher interest...they draw off of that energy." On the other hand, if students feel that the teacher does not care, they will not care enough to get into the activity.

Overall, the teachers interviewed seemed to feel that the activities they used required a lot of effort to plan, present, manage, and evaluate, regardless of the type of activity. One teacher praised discussion. "I take issues from my own reading of magazines and newspapers (which I would do anyway) and develop questions for discussion," she said. "I like it since it is fairly effortless. It is an activity out there waiting to happen." Another teacher, however, pointed out that activities still require the effort of motivating the students to respond and of keeping the discussion on track. As for other activities, lectures require effort because you are the "sage on the stage." Cooperative learning requires continual attention from the teacher to make adjustments so it works. Labs require a lot of planning, preparation, management, and cleanup. As one teacher put it, "Anything you do takes effort."

## RATIONALE FOR ACTIVITIES

The question of justifying the use of certain activities was of great interest to our research team, and we wondered if teachers not only had good justifications for using certain activities, but if they made those justifications clear to the students. We found that teachers often had typical reasons for using activities and that although the students knew these reasons, they were not often told them. One teacher even said she did not give the students reasons "because they already know."

The most interesting finding from our interviews was not the typicality of the justifications for activities. It was the sarcasm and apathy shown in students' responses to the question. Even after listing typical reasons such as "so you can understand," "so you can get along with others," "to learn the material," "because you're going to need this in the future," "because you can use this in everyday life," and "because it stimulates interaction, develops our social and communication skills, and helps us grasp ideas," students usually ended up saying "I don't really know why we do it" or "Most of the time they don't (give us reasons), they just say 'Hey, do this!'" They listed the "real" reasons why teachers use the activities they do as "because they're being paid to do it" and "because it's their job." A group of students commented, "Teachers have us do independent work because they are sick of us being loud. They are afraid that we will all socialize if we work together." They did soften this a little by commenting that teachers "have us work independently to provide an equal learning opportunity—they want all students to participate." "Some teachers really do want to help," a different group of students commented, but they then ended with more pessimism, "...but some don't care."

One student summed it all up. "It's tradition," she said. "School's tradition. You get a book; you study the chapter; you have a quiz; you move on to the next chapter and do the same thing." This seemed to be the overall feeling of all of the students interviewed. Even students who had, moments before, earnestly described situations where they "did it," "got it," had fun in the process, and felt proud of their accomplishments, did not see that process or that feeling as a justification for the activities. Students who praised group work or practice time because it allowed them to get their work done and get their questions answered did not mention these qualities as justifications for the use of the activities.

From the teacher's perspective, the rationale for using particular activities was less pessimistic. They saw the activities they used as encouraging basic learning skills, enhancing thinking skills, and providing practice for interpersonal skills. One teacher expressly mentioned "job-related skills and professionalism." One science teacher was more specific about discussions. "The goal of discussion and brainstorming is to get the students to think beyond their 16-year-old social life," she said. "I tell them this. What I often tell them is that before many years they will be faced with decisions like voting. Our discussion of some of these very contemporary issues will prepare them to be educated decisionmakers."

As good as the intentions of the teachers may be, their goals do not seem to be conveyed effectively either to students or administrators. One administrator seemed to be making excuses for the teachers when he stated, "It's part of their curriculum. Teachers get into a box and tend to not change." Again, the principal summed it all up quite well. He admitted that there were many occasions when activities were presented without any explanation or justification, and he felt that even some of the justifications that were given missed the mark because they did not have the correct correlation between value in the present and usefulness in the future. He stated that teachers were trying for more "life relevance" but admitted that that was hard to do. He ended with comments that seemed to echo the pessimistic note of the students. "It's part of the curriculum," he said. "We still do it because *that's the way we do it*." The vice-principal also agreed that teachers often communicate what students are to do but fail to explain why. She noted communication of objective as an area that needed improvement for the majority of the staff. She also noted that teachers do have reasons for doing activities that they feel are important, but they don't always tell the class.

Our research team found it truly interesting that this question produced the most pessimistic responses from students and some of the least inspired answers from teachers and administrators. It invites some further questions concerning the overall usefulness of our educational system and how students and society perceive it in general.

## EFFECTIVE TEACHING

Our final question was intended to provide a summary and a conclusion to our research. The responses we received were varied but similar. Students, teachers, and administrators all emphasized three key attributes of effective teaching: *variety*, *organization*, and *student involvement*.

As was already mentioned, variety is the most evident attribute of teaching and learning in a block period. Teachers must plan several activities that address the same concepts. To do this in a truly effective manner, the teacher must be organized. As one group of students put it, "Effective teaching is a class that runs smoothly, is well organized, and lasts for the whole period. An effective teacher does not just hand out worksheets; he or she is always prepared."

Students even had suggestions for the best way to organize activities. They liked to have a short review of material at the beginning of class with some time for questions to be answered. A quick lecture or instructions for a lab or activity should follow this. Then group work and individual practice time would take up the majority of the period. The period would end with a discussion and some instructions about how to prepare for the next day.

In addition to the themes of variety, organization, and in-volvement, there were specific suggestions for effective teaching. Students emphasized hands-on learning and one-on-one interactions with teachers. One student specifically requested "less students, more teachers." Others requested less work, but assignments that took longer to complete, emphasizing that in-depth work was better than just assigning double the amount of work that would be assigned in a shorter period. Again, issues of practice time and stretching lessons across several days were mentioned, and often students' comments ended up where they started. As one student put it, "An effective teacher should work more on in-depth thinking processes and teach more than one concept in a period— variety is key."

Teachers mentioned a general goal of three different activities per class period, all focused on the same set of concepts but coming at them from different angles and utilizing different learning styles. As with the students, teachers mentioned review, introduction of new material, individual practice and group work, and a final check for understanding as a good pattern to follow. One teacher summed up the issue of organization and planning as follows: "Ultimately, be prepared, since it is harder to 'wing it' in a 100-minute period." Even with the goals of variety and preparedness in mind, one teacher did point out a negative aspect of the longer period: "The danger with this system is that you may not cover enough or challenge enough." This comment illumines just how important use of time is in a 100-minute period system. For the use of time to be effective, it seems that one must be extremely well-prepared, for both the short-term and long-term, with activities that engage and challenge all learners.

The principal defined effective teaching in two parts. From an objective standpoint, effective teaching involves a clear-cut instructional objective that can be measured; class time appropriately divided into segments that involve some teacher-centered and some student-centered activities; and by the end, demonstrations that the students have met the objective. From a subjective standpoint, effective teaching is related to the "feel" of the classroom as the student enters and leaves.

This subjective "feel" was perhaps the most ambiguous way of defining effective teaching, but there were several other subjective measures of effectiveness. One teacher stated that his teaching was effective if the basic skill being taught was enhanced by the end of the period. Another judged the effectiveness of her teaching on the accomplishments of the students. She was effective, she believed, if she knew "that they've stretched, they've grown, they've taken risks, and they've gained some insight into human nature."

A student put the definition of effective teaching in a more personal perspective. She said, "To me, effective teaching is when they, like, take the time to explain it and they explain it good, in-depth." She added that it was not effective if the teacher did not know the concepts well enough to explain them. And she emphasized again that after the explanation, effective teachers "give you time to work on it, practice it."

In sum, the data suggest several themes as central to definitions of effectiveness in a 100-minute period. Variety was mentioned many times by teachers, administrators, and students. All three agreed that a variety of activities, if properly used, creates a learning opportunity that is effective as well as enjoyable. An effective teacher uses variety, but has carefully prepared the activities considering the needs and learning styles of the students. It seems that an effective teacher should devote a portion of the time to communicating the objectives of each activity to the students. Time is easier to structure if one is teaching to an objective and giving reasons helps students to see the purpose of each activity. Perhaps when students learn why they are being asked to engage in a given activity, the learning becomes more meaningful, and the activity can then be seen as more effective by all involved. Though these themes were clearly seen in all participants' responses, the variety of activities used is dependent upon the teacher and the content being taught. While all agree that variety and preparedness are important, how this variety is implemented looks very different from classroom to classroom.

## CONCLUSION AND ACTION PLAN

The primary message of our research in terms of its application to the classroom is *variety*. The fact that our discovered themes of *variety, organization,* and *involvement* are rather obvious does not make them any less important. As teachers, this discovery will push us to be more self-conscious of our own use of variety in the classroom. It focuses our attention on the need to plan different activities and transitions between activities to maximize our effectiveness in 100 minutes.

Our research also gives us clues about appropriate patterns for organizing activities in block periods. Both teachers and students mentioned review, lecture, group work and practice time, discussion and a check for understanding, and preparation for the next day as a useful general template for teaching in block periods. Our research shows a clear preference among students for large blocks of time devoted to group work and individual practice. These activities were not mentioned as much by teachers, and some teachers even questioned whether such activities were an efficient use of time. Our research clearly shows that students like it, so perhaps the next step is to find ways to insure that students achieve measurable goals during such activities and thereby provide justification for teachers to be comfortable using such activities.

Our research also serves as a reminder to teachers to be systematically reflective. As teachers, we must not only ask ourselves if a lesson was successful or not, but we must specifically bring the notion of time and variety into our self-critiques. We must focus on the proper balance between student-centered and teacher-centered activities, and we must achieve a balance between time devoted to group work and time used for individual practice. The common analogy that came up in our interviews with teachers, students, and administrators was that of a coach. We must focus on providing opportunities for guided practice in class so that students feel competent and comfortable doing the work we expect them do on their own.

The student input and reactions were extremely helpful to our study and very valuable to us as teachers. After the interviews with students got rolling, and they became more serious (moving past the "I like sitting around doing nothing" phase), the comments on specific activities as well as on general class time issues was very helpful. This process itself emphasized the importance of asking students to reflect seriously on classroom activities as they unfold, not just in an occasional study. Again, this area pushes us to be more specific in our reflection on our teaching. As teachers, we must set up an arena in which students are encouraged to critique the teaching and learning that occur in the classroom seriously and thoughtfully so that meaningful improvements can be made by both the teacher and students.

## IMPLICATIONS FOR FURTHER RESEARCH

As we began our research, we noted that there were many questions we could not hope to approach because we did not have any starting point from which to proceed. Specific questions about the effectiveness of certain activities were avoided because we did not have a definition of "effective." While our current research has made some progress in this area, it still seems that effectiveness is too vague a concept to be used to evaluate activities. Instead, separate objective and subjective measures of student involvement, student achievement, and student and teacher effort should be developed. In addition, summaries of the learning styles utilized in activities and investigations of how well different sequences of activities work would be useful for teacher planning and organization of classroom time.

Clearly, the questions we asked were very broad. This broadness led us to a large number of more specific inquiries. We are interested in the meeting place between variety, which is clearly very important, and ritual in the block-period classroom. How does the notion of ritual fit into the longer periods? Is it as important as variety? This question leads to others: Are there ITIP-styled "recipes" to be discovered in block-period lesson planning? Are there specific sequences of activities (outside of classroom rituals) that can be counted on to be effective in most teachers' hands, regardless of personal teaching style? Are different activities or sequences more or less effective depending on the subject area in which they are used? Are specific activities more effective than others are in the block period? A study of the use of a sole activity such as cooperative learning, discussion, or individual work, for example, may be an interesting and enlightening area for further study.

One final set of questions that arose within our research team was inspired by the youth of our team. While we have one member with 11 years experience in education, he is currently a counselor and therefore not in the classroom on a regular basis. Of the three other members, two are first-year teachers and one is in his second year. Our youth became an issue during the interviews. Those more experienced teachers whom we interviewed sometimes saw ideas we saw as widespread or common practice as radical change. This generational difference leads us to some final questions for further research. Is there a big difference between what teacher education programs present as "best practice" and the actual practice of established educators? Also, what are teacher education programs covering when it comes to preparing teachers for working in block-period days?

To conclude, the collaborative action research process is a rewarding method for looking at an issue that affects the context of teaching and attempting to see it from the different perspectives of the researchers as well as the interview participants. The study gave us insight into the importance of variety, organization, and student involvement in activities within a block period. The process helped us to be reflective about our own teaching practices in the never-ending quest to serve all students' best interests effectively and efficiently. And finally, the study taught us to remember to listen to what all members of the school culture have to say—teachers, administrators, and especially our students. The teachers and administrators appreciate that their opinions matter and that what they are doing is important. The students' voices ring with honesty and offer truthful accounts of what works for them if only we give them a chance to be heard.

(Ms. Alexander teaches mathematics and English. Mr. Lovre teaches English. Mr. Olson teaches physics and physical science. Mr. Smith is a school counselor.)

## CRITICAL COMMENTS

The following comments were written by David Marshak.

The Cedarcrest High School study illustrates several of the steps toward a new model of high school as described in Chapter 1. It also identifies several interesting avenues for further research.

According to the Cedarcrest data, only 11% of class time was devoted to whole-class direct instruction, presumably lecture. Looking at the breakdown by subject, the totals varied from 0% of class time in the arts to, at most, 18% in mathematics. These data support the idea that lecture is no longer the primary teaching method.

The totals from the Cedarcrest time survey are distorted somewhat by the inclusion of nearly twice as many minutes of instruction from vocational subjects as from English, mathematics, science, or physical education. This skewing requires that we look beyond the totals at each subject area. When we do, several findings emerge:

- Whole class discussion, which might or might not have a lecture-like quality to it depending on how discussion is defined, has a clear role in every subject, with a higher percentage of time in the academic subjects (from 12% in math to 18% in English) than in vocational classes or physical education.
- The role of individual practice, with an aggregate rating of 28% of class time, actually varies dramatically from vocational classes (47%) and physical education (55%) to academic classes such as mathematics (8%) and science (4%). Ex-

cept for science, the amount of time devoted to individual practice is similar to the amount of time given to whole class discussion in several subjects, including English, math, and the arts.

◆   Math devotes the least time to small group work (8%). In all other subjects, small group work ranges from significant (English at 20%, vocational and physical education both at 19%) to central (science at 44% and the arts at 60%).

◆   English, math, and science classes provide students with a significant amount of time to work on homework in class. The report that 24% of class time in English is devoted to homework raises questions about appropriate time use in these classes. The report that 30% of class time in mathematics classes is devoted to testing raises similar questions.

The Cedarcrest researchers comment, "From the perspective of the teacher, the more the students are involved in an activity, the more worthwhile the activity seems to be." While this is clearly an impressionistic conclusion drawn from interview data, it suggests that the interviewed teachers have begun to move into a model of high school that seeks not passivity and compliance from students but that views student activity as central to the value of their work as teachers.

The researchers note that "overlapping lessons that continue for two periods or longer may be more effective." This hypothesis identifies the need for further research into the questions of how student learning is affected both by block-period instruction and by the various block-period schedules.

The researchers explain, "This seemed to be the overall feeling of all of the students interviewed. Even students who had, moments before, earnestly described situations where they 'did it,' 'got it,' had fun in the process, and felt proud of their accomplishments did not see that process or that feeling as a justification for the activities....One student summed it all up. 'It's tradition,' she said. 'School's tradition. You get a book;

you study the chapter; you have a quiz; you move on to the next chapter and do the same thing....' They listed the 'real' reasons why teachers use the activities they do as 'because they're being paid to do it' and 'because it's their job.'"

We can view these accounts as evidence that Cedarcrest is a school in transition from the conventional model to something different. Many teachers at the school have begun to teach in a nonconventional way. It is the particulars of this teaching to which students are responding with engagement, enthusiasm, and appreciation. Yet these same teachers may not have moved far enough into a different vision and structure of high school either to communicate the purposes and objectives of activities to students on a regular basis or to involve students in helping to set the course of their own learning.

The researchers themselves seem to understand their own situation at Cedarcrest when they write:

> This process [action research] itself emphasized the importance of asking students to reflect seriously on classroom activities as they unfold, not just in an occasional study. Again, this area pushes us to be more specific in our reflection on our teaching. As teachers, we must set up an arena in which students are encouraged to critique the teaching and learning that occur in the classroom seriously and thoughtfully so that meaningful improvements can be made by both the teacher and students.

The enactment of the activities described in this statement would move at least these particular teachers deeply into a new model of high school.

# APPENDIX 5.1. LIST OF CLASSROOM ACTIVITIES

The following list of classroom activities was compiled from the results of our initial survey of teachers during a faculty meeting. Teachers were simply asked to write down all the instructional activities which occurred in their classroom.

Application
Attendance
Audio Tape
Book
Brainstorm
Circuit Learning/Training
Class Work
CNN
Computer Technology
Cooperative Learning
Current Events
Demonstration
Diagrams
Discipline Intervention
Discovery Learning
Discussion
Evaluation
Evaluation (Student)
Evaluation (Verbal)
Evaluation (Written)
Example (Direct)
Example (inferred)
Field Study
Field Trip
Film Strip
Films
Games
Group Work
Guided Practice
Hands On

Independent Practice
Independent Work
Individual Development
Individual Work
Interactive Lecture
Journal Writing
Lab Work
Lecture
Metacognition (Thinking Skills)
Multi-Media
Outdoor Activity
Performances
Posters
Pre/Post Tests
Presentations
Projects
Question/Answer
Quizzes
Reading
Research
Review
Role-Play
Seat Work
Station Learning/Training
Student Sharing
Student Teaching
Tests
Tutorial (Individual)
Tutorial (Small Group)
Video (Interactive)
Video Time
Visual Aids
Walks

## APPENDIX 5.2. TRACKING CLASSROOM ACTIVITIES

Date _____

Period ___

# of students in class ____

Grade level _____

Subject discipline _____

Please rate this week as

Atypical  1  2  3  4  5  Very typical

For one week, please track the classroom activities which occurred in one of your courses.

Use the back of this sheet for any necessary explanations

The attached sheet contains a list of the classroom activities and techniques which teachers listed during the recent faculty meeting. This list is provided simply for reference.

|          | Monday | Tuesday | Wednesday | Thursday | Friday |
|----------|--------|---------|-----------|----------|--------|
| 0 min    |        |         |           |          |        |
| 20 min   |        |         |           |          |        |
| 40 min   |        |         |           |          |        |
| 60 min   |        |         |           |          |        |
| 80 min   |        |         |           |          |        |
| 100 min  |        |         |           |          |        |

Any other things you would like to tell us about your classroom would be appreciated (for example, classroom layout, classroom routines, specific classroom expectations, classroom materials, technology used, etc.). Please use the back of this sheet.               **Please return this sheet to Anthony Smith's mailbox.**

## APPENDIX 5.3. RESULTS OF THE TIME SURVEY

| Category | Total minutes | Percentage |
|---|---|---|
| Large Group Direct Instruction | 670 | 11% |
| Class Discussion | 640 | 10% |
| Small Group Work, Labs, Research | 1540 | 25% |
| Individual Practice | 1720 | 28% |
| Tests and Quizzes | 605 | 10% |
| Correcting Assignments | 260 | 4% |
| Homework, Reading | 460 | 7% |
| Videos, Audio Tape | 320 | 5% |
| Total | 6215 | |

**Table 2**
**Results of the Time Survey**
**by Subject Area**

| | Eng | Math | Sci | Voc | P.E. | Arts |
|---|---|---|---|---|---|---|
| Direct Instruction | 7% | 18% | 8% | 13% | 11% | 0% |
| Discussion | 18% | 12% | 14% | 6% | 6% | 10% |
| Sm. Group | 20% | 8% | 44% | 19% | 19% | 60% |
| Individual | 18% | 8% | 4% | 47% | 55% | 10% |
| Tests | 11% | 30% | 10% | 5% | 2% | 0% |
| Correcting | 2% | 10% | 4% | 5% | 0% | 0% |
| Homework | 24% | 14% | 10% | 0% | 0% | 0% |
| Videos | 0% | 0% | 7% | 5% | 7% | 20% |
| Total minutes | 900 | 1000 | 1000 | 1990 | 825 | 500 |

# APPENDIX 5.4. INTERVIEW QUESTIONS

## Interview Questions

### Student:
1. What classroom activities do you enjoy? Why?
2. What classroom activities do you find effective? How do you know they are effective?
3. How much effort do you have to put into these activities? What kind of effort? How does the effort involved relate to your feelings about the activity?
4. What reasons does the teacher give for doing these activities? Why do you think the teacher is having you do these activities?
5. How often are these activities actually used? Do you think they should be used more or less?
6. How do you define effective teaching in 100 minute period?

### Teacher:
1. What classroom activities do you enjoy? Why?
2. What classroom activities do you find effective? How do you know they are effective?
3. How much effort do you have to put into these activities? What kind of effort? How does the effort involved relate to your feelings about the activity?
4. What do you think the goals of these activities are? What reasons do you give the students for doing these activities?
5. How often are these activities actually used? Do you think they should be used more or less?
6. How do you define effective teaching in 100 minute period?

### Administrator:
1. What classroom activities do you enjoy seeing in the classroom? Why?
2. What classroom activities do you find effective? How do you know they are effective?
3. How much effort is involved in these activities? What kind of effort? How does the effort involved relate to your feelings about the activity?
4. What reasons does the teacher give to the students for doing these activities? Why do you think the teacher is having the students do these activities?
5. How often are these activities actually used? Do you think they should be used more or less?
6. How do you define effective teaching in 100 minute period?

# 6

# TAHOMA HIGH SCHOOL
## CONNECTED LEARNING IN BLOCK PERIODS

Kimberly Allison, Elizabeth Mathewson,
Mark Oglesby, Marianne Winter

### SCHOOL PORTRAIT AND INTRODUCTION

Tahoma High School, a four-year school, has an enrollment of 1,160 students and serves a predominantly rural area 30 miles southeast of Seattle. About 6 percent of the students are persons of color.

Tahoma High School is in its second year of a block-period schedule. The faculty, with a team of parents and students, investigated block periods during the 1992–93 academic year, and during the spring of that year, selected a three-period day plan to begin with the 1994–95 academic year. The three-period schedule (Blue Day periods 1, 2, 3; Gold Day periods 4, 5, 6) caused the least impact on existing class offerings, especially electives, and on contact time per credit. Thus, students are still registered for six courses, which did not change how scheduling had been done in the past. In the intervening academic year, 1993–94, the entire staff was taught active learning strategies in eight half-day sessions. Active learning strategies are ones that elicit high levels of student involvement in the learning process.

The three instructors for these eight sessions were selected by the principal from the faculty itself. These teachers had at least 15 years of teaching experience and the principal had observed them consistently incorporating active learning strategies in their lessons. Before each of the eight early release days, these three instructors were each given a release day from their classrooms to plan. Quality space, equipment, time, and secretarial support were provided to put together the in-services. Nancy Skerritt, the head of the district's Curriculum and Instruction Office, served as a mentor to these teachers and was frequently present as an advisor for these planning sessions.

At the eight in-services, faculty members actually became students again, this time in simulated block periods, as they were introduced to and practiced the active learning strategies that they would be using with their own students. Providing a year for teachers to incorporate new active learning strategies into their existing procedures was thought beneficial for changing instruction and assuring a smoother move into block periods.

At the final session of these eight half-days, each staff member was given THE FILE, a binder containing information presented in the sessions, and articles and materials easily copied for use in the classroom. Some instructional strategies included in THE FILE were cooperative learning, multiple intelligences, graphic organizers for teaching thinking skills, self-reflection and assessment suggestions, and a lesson design tool that offered, at a glance, multiple strategies to engage students actively in the learning process. In addition to THE FILE, each teacher received a copy of *Inspiring Active Learning* by Merrill Harmin (Alexandria, VA: ASCD, 1994). This is a handbook providing multiple strategies to move a teacher into a facilitator-of-learning role rather than the giver-of-all-knowledge role.

For 7 years prior to the move to block periods, the principal at Tahoma High School was an energized visionary who encouraged change. Under her tenure, schoolwide daily sustained silent reading was begun; a daily, afterschool homework center staffed by teachers was designed; a three-part senior project required for all graduating seniors was started; and a pilot program integrating social studies, science, and English for 90 9th graders was designed. (All Tahoma students are placed in English and social studies blocks in 7th and 8th grades.)

An entire year was taken to plan this 9th-grade integrated program. This popular integrated program, driven thematically by science, is taught by three teachers who have common planning time and frequently meet with all 90 students together. A team planned a similar sophomore program to begin the following year so the same 90 9th graders and their teachers moved into the 10th grade together. A new group of 9th graders began the integrated program the following year. Several teachers at Tahoma High School, who do not work directly with the integrated program, have formed temporary teams, and have taken a 24-hour class in curriculum integration at the district office. It is intended that each year additional teams will be given release from the teaching day to take these classes in integrating curriculum.

In August of the year block periods were to begin, the principal left the district. Although this caused some anxiety, the staff moved ahead with the block periods under the principalship of an interim administrator. The first year in block periods, 1994–95, two of the teachers from the original instructional team were given a consulting period, a period free of student responsibility, so they could provide individual instructional support to teachers requesting help with the block periods. The eight half-day in-service sessions that first year of block periods provided opportunities for teachers to synthesize and assimilate the strategies taught the year before. Staff met and shared their discoveries in interdepartmental groups of six to eight people and in departmental groups. Staff members who had developed especially exciting programs for the block periods taught six mini-sessions the final half-day of that first year. The second year in block periods, 1995–96, the eight half-day inservice sessions again provided time for staff to work on self-selected teams collaborating in curriculum development.

Two principal factors led to our collaborative action research team's curiosity about connected learning. First, a new creative energy and excitement for integrating curriculum pervades the staff since the introduction of the 100-minute periods. Because 16 early release days over the past 2 years have focused on collaborative curriculum development and active learning strategies, the faculty has moved out of the isolation of its departmental towers and into conversations about curriculum integration.

The second factor leading to our curiosity about connected learning is the placement of 90 11th-graders from the integrated 9th and 10th pilot programs into six isolated subjects again. In these six subjects, separated by department, students must make their own connections. They miss the rich educational opportunities they experienced during their first 2 years of high school. Science, English, and social studies are closely connected to the real world, and in integrated program classes, many lessons take place in that world. Six staff members are intimately knowledgeable and excited about the connections that occur in this integrated program, and their excitement has influenced other staff to consider developing an integrated 11th-grade program.

Except for the integrated 9th and 10th block, the school and curriculum is arranged in a traditional department format. With the block periods and the increased collaborative planning opportunities available in half days, teachers have undoubtedly discovered new active learning strategies, and we were curious to discover how much awareness of connected learning existed for both faculty and students in school and outside of school.

## RESEARCH METHODOLOGY

We first asked our faculty to define connected learning using an exit slip format. Combining the commonalities of the definitions suggested, we created our own four-part definition:

- Linking past, present, and future learnings and experiences
- Bridging and building concepts and ideas between content areas
- Raising consciousness about the importance of the interconnections

♦ Raising awareness that life is an intricate web of connections

Using this definition, we surveyed a random group of 20 teachers (15 were regular and special education classroom teachers and 5 taught in our integrated language arts-science-social studies program). This survey (see Appendix 6.1) asked teachers to respond to eight questions regarding the role of connected learning in their own lives, the value of connected learning in education, and strategies for and evidence of connected learning in their classrooms.

After collecting and analyzing this data, we created a student survey based on the same four-part definition of connected learning (see Appendices 6.2–6.5). Ninth through twelfth graders were polled, as well as a mix from traditional classrooms and our integrated program. We then compared and contrasted the data from teachers and students focusing on four areas:

♦ The perceived value and importance of connected learning

♦ Connected learning in block periods

♦ Connected learning and the integrated program

♦ Strategies for connected learning

## FINDINGS AND ANALYSIS

### THE VALUE OF CONNECTED LEARNING

Overall, teachers reported that connected learning was not only a relevant and necessary aid to their own learning but also a requirement for meaningful and relevant learning in the classroom. One teacher responded, "Teachers *must* be able to make subject matter relevant to students' lives, regardless of the topic. If we teach students to make connections on their own by modeling and demonstration, they will hopefully be more excited about learning and use what they've learned." Repeatedly, teachers affirmed the importance of connected learning with statements suggesting that "real learning" could not occur without connections. All of the teachers we surveyed valued connected learning, but some expressed a lack of the skills and strategies necessary to make connected learning happen in their classrooms. Along that line, one teacher stressed that connected learning was "too important a skill to leave to chance." Teachers had an easy time citing specific examples of connected learning in their own lives, but many confided that their awareness of the importance of connected learning didn't come until college and even then, it was by chance.

Students had a more difficult time recognizing classes where connected learning was stressed. Many, especially seniors, only valued connected learning insofar as they saw the content related to their lives. With seniors, the "world of work" was especially important. Students seemed less able to make connections between content areas except in the case of the students currently involved in our integrated program. The integrated-program students seemed both to value connected learning and to be able to recognize when it happened. However, many expressed a lack of desire to make the connections themselves. When forced to use connected learning, as with an assignment, students in the integrated program felt they could make connections on their own, yet they did not necessarily choose to do so. In traditional classrooms, students said little specifically about the importance of connected learning beyond how classes connect to their lives. We were surprised, however, by the number of students who cited math as their most relevant subject, because as one student said, "Math is everything." These students did not provide evidence for why math was so important, and we began to suspect our math department has a good public relations program going. Other students cited keyboarding, traffic safety, and other hands-on courses that seemed to bridge the gap between school and the real world in a very concrete way.

## CONNECTED LEARNING IN BLOCK PERIODS

One of our goals was to find out if block periods were conducive to connected learning. As expected, the teachers believe block periods provide more time and opportunity for learning. Since students learn at different rates and with different styles, the extra time allows for a variety of ways to move beyond the content to the connections. For some teachers, block periods are the only opportunity "to bring out connections between classroom study and experiences outside of the classroom." Projects, group discussions, and individual attention are a few of the strategies teachers use to allow students to make connections between content areas and life experiences.

Students like the opportunities that block periods offer them, as well. One senior said she could "focus for a greater period of time on one subject, allowing for freer flowing thoughts and higher chances of internal connections being made." An underclassman likes the ability for "discussion about ideas and how they relate to the world around us." Very few students had negative comments about the block periods, and those who did were often procrastinators. Students who enjoyed the extra time for homework offset this. Most of the responses were favorable toward the extra time to extend learning and therefore connected learning.

The teachers and students are in agreement concerning the value of the block periods. More than 75 percent of the staff and more than 50 percent of the students prefer the block periods to the standard schedule. Both groups believe the time and opportunity for discussion is invaluable.

## INTEGRATED CURRICULUM AND CONNECTED LEARNING

One clear benefit of the block periods is that they allow for more flexibility in planning for curriculum integration. In surveying teachers, we found that integration is valued and individuals would like to see more of it. Currently, at Tahoma High School, six teachers are directly involved with the 9th- and 10th-grade integrated science, social studies, and English program. However, many other teachers are planning integrated units within their content areas or teaming with other teachers for short units they planned during the eight half-days.

Teachers expressed a strong support for integration. One stated, "Students are able to build bridges more easily and connect the learnings more easily." Integration provides students with opportunities to see connections, not just hear about them. Another teacher commented, "Students have the ability to see connections between content in integrated classes whereas traditional students must oftentimes be lead." Clearly, integration is seen as a tool to improve student learning.

Several strategies for integration were mentioned in the teacher survey. These included basing the curriculum on current issues, thereby allowing students to see how everything is interrelated in the world. Also, English teachers have found that by using language arts skills such as speaking, listening, reading, and text interpretation to look at current issues, their essential learnings are a natural fit with other more content-specific courses. This flexibility often allows other more content-specific classes to drive the curriculum. For example, the 9th- and 10th-grade programs are driven by science, and social studies and language arts dovetail by discussing, writing, and reading about the relevant social, environmental, and political concepts.

The strongest argument in support of integration, however, is reflected in the students' comments on their surveys. In fact, the students' comments were even more revealing and specific than were the teachers. *Students repeatedly responded that integration makes learning easier, more relevant, and better.* The benefits of an integrated class that students mentioned included teachers coordinating homework, group problem solving, and the weaving of big concepts together to aid in understanding. Students enjoyed the real-life applications and generally felt they were getting a better education. They cited a better understanding of news and current events as evidence that they were learning more and making connections. Students also responded that their metacognition skills increased. One freshman said, "You can't not learn in Integrated." A junior who had spent 2 years in the integrated program stated, "I learned how I learned, and I constantly realize how much I know from Integrated that other students from traditional programs don't." Students also felt that the block periods and integration "created strong friendship bonds with classmates and teachers alike." On an attitudinal note, several students noted that they felt calmer on integrated days and that classes went smoother because all of their teachers were talking about similar concepts. Strategies that the students mentioned included group work, providing examples, and writing across the curriculum.

Through our surveys, it has become clear that the block periods allow for more integration of curriculum and students and teachers value that integration. This kind of curriculum integration is a direction in which we want to head.

## STRATEGIES FOR CONNECTED LEARNING

### *TEACHER RESPONSES TO SURVEY REGARDING STRATEGIES USED TO CONNECT LEARNING*

See Appendix 6.1 for the questions. Figures in parentheses are multiple similar responses to a question.

- ◆ Strategies must be student driven.
- ◆ The teacher should serve as coach.
- ◆ The teacher models connected learning. (3)
- ◆ Connected learning cannot be force-fed.
- ◆ As teachers, we must force kids to create metaphors to compare and contrast something new or unusual. What does "X" remind you of? (2)
- ◆ Connected learning can be taught by demonstration, valuing connections, and teaching thinking skills and thinking behaviors.
- ◆ Connected learning can be fostered by frequently relating current events to the classroom. (3)
- ◆ The teacher must construct an environment to foster connected learning. (4)

- Mistakes by students are welcomed as opportunities to further connected thinking.
- The teacher must provide opportunities to journal, self-reflect, and extrapolate for connected learning. (4)
- For connected learning to work we must build frameworks for kids to hang their learning on.
- We must build on prior knowledge.
- To foster connected learning we must construct multidimensional projects or lessons in our content-specific classrooms.
- Give extra credit to students who announce connections from the classroom to their lives outside of the classroom. (2)
- Discuss possibilities of career opportunities as they relate to classwork.
- I announce connected learnings from Spanish to English.
- Teaching the multiple intelligences fosters connected learning.

## TEACHER STRATEGIES MENTIONED IN STUDENT RESPONSES FROM NONINTEGRATED CLASSES

See Appendices 6.2–6.5 for the questions. Figures in parentheses are multiple similar responses to a question.

- Writing and speaking help us to get connected to other ideas, places, and people's ideas. (4)
- Connected learning is helped when teachers tell us we need something for another class or the next class in a series.
- Connected learning occurs when teachers give us more time to process, ask questions, and get individual help.

- Teachers seem to be doing a more thoughtful job preparing lessons for connected learning.
- Agriculture and horticulture lessons are planned well to include lots of activities.
- It seems that upper classmen have a greater variety of classes to choose from that relate to areas of interest they are pursuing.
- Longer periods are more boring and we can lose our focus. (2)
- Sitting in small groups helps us practice communication.
- Writing position papers helps us learn to take a stand and defend it.
- Discussion opportunities help us connect to other areas.

## RESPONSES TO STUDENT SURVEY OF STUDENTS IN INTEGRATED PROGRAM

See Appendices 6.2–6.5 for the questions.

- We learn more from updated relevant stuff, not old textbooks.
- The teachers made connections and showed the importance of what was being learned and why one would want to know the information.
- The teachers showed how the information we learned was related to people's lives and current times.
- We study current political issues, real world.
- Lots of activities.
- Because we talk about news issues in Integrated, I pay more attention to them outside of class.
- When I read a newspaper, I make connections to things I have learned in school.

- We stay on the same topic from class to class instead of changing constantly.
- I know how to make connections, but don't do it on my own.
- Generally, 9th-grade students do not feel confident about making connections on their own.
- In Integrated, we bonded student to student, student to teacher, and this made learning easier.
- The teachers taught problem-solving techniques and organizational methods.

## ACTION PLAN

One research question we hoped to answer was, "Can direct instruction of connected learning impact student skills?" Unfortunately, we didn't gain much new information in this area. Therefore, we want to continue to work with this idea by trying and sharing strategies for connected learning. Because we found that both teachers and students highly value connected learning, we believe it is important to pursue this issue wholeheartedly.

Another area of focus for our school is adding new integrated courses to the class offerings at Tahoma. Our research thoroughly validated the concept of integration. Both teachers and learners are excited about the type of education that takes place in integrated courses. We see a need for a variety of integrated courses that are driven by teacher compatibility and student desires. We believe the intentional connections that can be made in integrated courses are valuable for all those involved. For example, a team has been selected to coordinate and develop an American Studies course that integrates U.S. History and American Expressions (an integrated composition and literature course).

Our research affirmed the value of block periods and integrated curriculum in the perceptions of teachers and students. Our district is fortunate to have already tried so many creative educational practices. With any new or innovative technique, we feel there is a great need for time for discussion, collaboration, and reflection.

Within our integration, we would also like to focus on the thinking skills of metacognition as they relate to making connections. We would like to increase the perceived value of these skills and the awareness of their importance. Just as we have found favorable results with direct instruction of thinking skills and multiple intelligences, making connections must also be presented and directly taught as a set of valuable skills.

With more integration and making connections, it is our intent that the distinct and fragmented content barriers that exist within a high school faculty and class schedule may diminish. All classes should reinforce real life connections and connections between content areas. Students perceive the study of "real life" events as valuable. Therefore, the use of the newspaper is a valuable resource. Also, students proved that they valued direct career connections. Therefore, it is our aim to make teaching broad connections and the skills involved with teaching in this way the focus of our school's curriculum.

(Ms. Allison and Ms. Mathewson teach English. Ms. Winter teaches English and related studies in the Integrated Program. Mr. Oglesby teaches social studies.)

## CRITICAL COMMENTS

David Marshak wrote the following comments.

In this study, the four teacher-researchers from Tahoma High School enacted a model of the way that action research can enrich teaching practice as well as the literature of teaching. From their experience they identified a category of phenomena, which they eventually decided to call connected learning. When they searched the literature for relevant citations, they found only a few marginally useful documents. Rather than withdraw from this line of inquiry, they engaged their faculty colleagues in helping to invent and define their own category. With this work complete, they set out to explore the nature of their category: connected learning.

The researchers note, "Students seemed less able to make connections between content areas except in the case of the students currently involved in our integrated program. The integrated-program students seemed both to value connected learning and to be able to recognize when it happened." This conclusion, clearly drawn, though somewhat tentative, suggests that the integrated-program classrooms are enacting a different kind of high school education than are the regular ones. "A junior who had spent 2 years in the integrated program stated, 'I learned how I learned, and I constantly realize how much I know from Integrated that other students from traditional programs don't.'" This student's description suggests a more personalized education in which self-knowledge has a role. It also suggests a more active role for the student in the learning process.

The researchers also note, "However, many [students] expressed a lack of desire to make the connections themselves. When 'forced' to use connected learning, as with an assignment, students in the integrated program felt they could make connections on their own, yet they did not necessarily choose to do so." One hypothesis to explain this phenomenon is that a year or two in a program that is moving toward a different model of school is not enough to shift the majority of students from a passive, receiving set to an active, creating orientation. Many students had learned this new set of thinking skills, but they hadn't yet consistently accepted responsibility for using them. If accurate, this analysis raises the question of how much opportunity students have in the integrated classroom to set the directions for their own learning. Is the message clear that their own thinking matters and can impact what happens in school? Or are they receiving a mixed message in that teachers encourage them to think in a connected way but also present them with a relatively fixed, unchangeable curriculum?

The researchers explain:

> Since students learn at different rates and with different styles, the extra time [in block periods] allows for a

variety of ways to move beyond the content to the connections. For some teachers, block periods are the only opportunity "to bring out connections between classroom study and experiences outside of the classroom." Projects, group discussions, and individual attention are a few of the strategies teachers use to allow students to make connections between content areas and life experiences.

Here the researchers describe some new elements that have become part of teaching practice at Tahoma: engagement of a variety of learning activities; an implied movement from coverage of a set curriculum toward an understanding that the curriculum explored within the classroom needs to be connected to phenomena and experiences outside the classroom if it is to have meaning for students; and an implicit recognition that perceived meaning, as gauged by the level of student involvement, is important in the high school classroom.

One teacher commented, "Students have the ability to see connections between content in integrated classes whereas traditional students must oftentimes be lead." The work of these teacher-researchers at Tahoma suggests that we may need to expand the list of elements within a new model of high school to include integrated curriculum and connected learning.

## APPENDIX 6.1. TEACHER SURVEY

GIVEN THAT *CONNECTED LEARNING* IS:

* LINKING PAST, PRESENT AND FUTURE LEARNINGS AND EXPERIENCES
* BRIDGING AND BUILDING CONCEPTS/IDEAS BETWEEN CONTENT AREAS
* RAISING CONSCIOUSNESS TO IMPORTANCE OF THE INTERCONNECTIONS
* RAISING AWARENESS THAT LIFE IS AN INTRICATE WEB OF CONNECTIONS

1. In your own life, how important is connected learning? How and when did you learn to make connections?

2. Is connected learning an important responsibility of education? Explain.

3. Can students make connections on their own?

4. Can direct instruction of connected learning impact student skills?

5. What kind of consideration, if any, do you give to connected learning when designing your lessons?

6. What specific strategies do you use to help students to make connections to your content area?

7. Does the extended period schedule allow for better student connected learning? Explain.

## APPENDIX 6.2. FRESHMAN STUDENT SURVEY

Freshman Survey

GIVEN THAT *CONNECTED LEARNING* IS:

* LINKING PAST, PRESENT AND FUTURE LEARNINGS AND EXPERIENCES
* BRIDGING AND BUILDING CONCEPTS/IDEAS BETWEEN CONTENT AREAS
* RAISING CONSCIOUSNESS TO IMPORTANCE OF THE INTERCONNECTIONS
* RAISING AWARENESS THAT LIFE IS AN INTRICATE WEB OF CONNECTIONS

1. Think about all of the classes you have taken at Tahoma High School. Did any of these classes prompt you to make connections between the content and other areas of your life? Please provide examples.

2. Learning was: (circle all that relate) easier, more relevant, better, the same in these classes because.....

3. Do the extended periods lend themselves to making better connections? Compare the two schedules in relation to connected learning.

IF YOU ARE IN THE INTEGRATED PROGRAM PLEASE COMPLETE THE FOLLOWING QUESTIONS.

4. Compare your integrated classes with your blue days in terms of making connections. Please provide examples of similarities and differences.

5. Do you feel that you are able to make connections on your own and do you do so? Please provide examples.

## APPENDIX 6.3. SOPHOMORE STUDENT SURVEY

Sophomore Survey

GIVEN THAT *CONNECTED LEARNING* IS:

* LINKING PAST, PRESENT AND FUTURE LEARNINGS AND EXPERIENCES
* BRIDGING AND BUILDING CONCEPTS/IDEAS BETWEEN CONTENT AREAS
* RAISING CONSCIOUSNESS TO IMPORTANCE OF THE INTERCONNECTIONS
* RAISING AWARENESS THAT LIFE IS AN INTRICATE WEB OF CONNECTIONS

1. Think about all of the classes you have taken at Tahoma High School. Did any of these classes prompt you to make connections between the content and other areas of your life? Please provide examples.

2. Learning was: (circle all that relate) easier, more relevant, better, the same in these classes because.....

3. Do the extended periods lend themselves to making better connections? Compare the two schedules in relation to connected learning.

IF YOU ARE IN THE INTEGRATED PROGRAM PLEASE COMPLETE THE FOLLOWING QUESTIONS.

4. Compare your integrated classes with your blue days in terms of making connections. Please provide examples of similarities and differences.

5. Do you feel that you are able to make connections on your own and will you be able to do so next year in your classes? what are some of the strategies you will use?

## APPENDIX 6.4. JUNIOR STUDENT SURVEY

Junior Survey

GIVEN THAT *CONNECTED LEARNING* IS:

* LINKING PAST, PRESENT AND FUTURE LEARNINGS AND EXPERIENCES
* BRIDGING AND BUILDING CONCEPTS/IDEAS BETWEEN CONTENT AREAS
* RAISING CONSCIOUSNESS TO IMPORTANCE OF THE INTERCONNECTIONS
* RAISING AWARENESS THAT LIFE IS AN INTRICATE WEB OF CONNECTIONS

1. With the exception of the integrated program, think about all of the classes you have taken at Tahoma High School. Did any of these classes prompt you to make connections between the content and other areas of your life? Please provide examples.

2. Learning was: (circle all that relate) easier, more relevant, better, the same in these classes because.....

3. Do the extended periods lend themselves to making better connections? Compare the two schedules in relation to connected learning.

IF YOU WERE A PART OF THE INTEGRATED PROGRAM, PLEASE COMPLETE THE FOLLOWING QUESTIONS.

4. Did the integrated program prompt you to make connections between content and other areas of your life? Examples?

5. Learning was: (circle all that relate) easier, more relevant, better, the same in these classes because ....

6. Do you apply the skills you learned in the integrated program to your classes this year? If so, how? Please be specific.

## APPENDIX 6.5. SENIOR STUDENT SURVEY

Senior Survey

GIVEN THAT *CONNECTED LEARNING* IS:

* LINKING PAST, PRESENT AND FUTURE LEARNINGS AND EXPERIENCES
* BRIDGING AND BUILDING CONCEPTS/IDEAS BETWEEN CONTENT AREAS
* RAISING CONSCIOUSNESS TO IMPORTANCE OF THE INTERCONNECTIONS
* RAISING AWARENESS THAT LIFE IS AN INTRICATE WEB OF CONNECTIONS

1. Think about all of the classes you have taken at Tahoma High School. Did any of these classes prompt you to make connections between the content and other areas of your life? Please provide examples.

2. Learning was: (circle all that relate) easier, more relevant, better, the same in these classes because.....

3. Do the extended periods lend themselves to making better connections? Compare the two schedules in relation to connected learning.

# 7

# DECATUR HIGH SCHOOL
## THE USE OF GROUP WORK IN 100-MINUTE PERIODS

MaryLee Heslop, Rick Hiser
Linda Kristin Reed, Chris Marquez

## SCHOOL PORTRAIT AND INTRODUCTION

Decatur High School, serving grades 10 through 12, is located in Federal Way, Washington, midway between Seattle and Tacoma. Of the 1,200 students at Decatur, 27 percent are persons of color. Federal Way is an economically diverse suburb, with housing ranging from low-income apartments to homes along the country club golf course.

Since September 1993, Decatur has operated on a three-period, alternating day schedule. Periods 1, 3, and 5 meet one day followed by 2, 4, and 6 the next. Each class meets for 100 minutes. Also, there are classes offered before and after school. The decision to adopt this longer-period schedule culminated a year of late-arrival day staff meetings in which a variety of schedules and educational innovations were explored. At the same time that we began the block-period schedule, the staff endorsed a "Career Paths" orientation to focus the students on future career choices and the courses that would begin to prepare them for their chosen career. Committees were formed to address altered-day scheduling, career paths, and accountability.

It was hoped that students would gain useful skills in their courses that would be more relevant to their future needs.

There had been a growing climate of violence and frustration in the school as the student population became more ethnically diverse and mobile. Longer periods would offer fewer passing times for students to confront each other in the hallways. At the same time, three classes per day meant fewer daily preparations for students and teachers. It was hoped that the longer class periods would provide the extra time needed for individual attention to promote understanding and reduce frustration. In fact, violence has been reduced, and the school climate is much more relaxed. Teacher, student, and parent comments indicate favorable responses to the block-period schedule. No teacher wants to return to the six-period day format. In addition, test scores on standardized tests have steadily improved.

Current issues related to block periods include integrated curriculum; curriculum adaptations to incorporate career skills; development and implementation of community partnerships; and the impact of alternating-day contact on first-year world language classes and music classes. Teachers would like to have more time to collaborate with colleagues to develop cross-curricular courses. To do this, they need release time and funds; therefore, opportunities are limited. Even in their own courses, teachers need time to develop and incorporate career-oriented materials. These materials may not be specifically oriented to one career but rather teach skills that would apply to various aspects of the world of work. Such skills include group cooperation and negotiation strategies as well as the use of technology and information sources for the production of final products. In addition, it is hoped that teachers will establish partnerships with the business community to add more relevance to their courses.

Scheduling also seems to be a limiting factor. The teachers of first-year world language courses have noticed a drop in the performance of their students in relation to the acquisition and retention of vocabulary and language structures. One Japanese teacher works part-time in a traditionally scheduled school, and he is the strongest advocate for daily contact between teachers and first-year language students. A modified schedule was proposed which would have paired first-year language classes with either history or English classes. Each of these paired classes would meet daily for 50 minutes. The number of students involved included only one-sixth of the student population. However, this revision was rejected by the administration for placing too many restrictions on the overall schedule.

## RESEARCH METHODOLOGY

We began by introducing the action research project to the faculty at the October late-arrival faculty meeting. After the introduction, we surveyed the faculty hoping to find a direction for our research (see Appendix 7.1, the Faculty Survey form). In addition to surveying the faculty, each member of our team surveyed her or his own students concerning 100-minute periods. We then formulated our research question, which the survey results and our own experience indicated should focus on group work in the 100-minute class period. Our research question was, *What does group work look like in the 100-minute period?*

Next, it was necessary to design the tools the committee would use to explore the nature of group work in the 100-minute class period. We decided to use three methods of data collection:

- ◆ a teacher interview to determine the teacher's description of group work within his or her classroom (see Appendix 7.2);

- ◆ a classroom observation of each interviewed teacher's 100-minute class during a time when students were engaged in group work (see Appendix 7.3); and

- ◆ a survey of students enrolled in the classes observed, so we could assess student attitudes toward group work and activities in the classroom (see Appendix 7.4).

Initially, each member of the research team observed another member of the team. This activity allowed us to test and

improve our three data collection instruments. We then observed 13 other teachers in the building.

# FINDINGS AND ANALYSIS

## CLASSROOM OBSERVATIONS

We found that each teacher we observed used small-group
discussion activities and that the work for each group was cur-
riculum-specific. Most teachers used small groups of three to
four students. In the *Annual* class where larger groups of four
to six students were used, some students observed were off-
task. Most of the classes observed were engaged in some type
of application activity that was a follow-up to the teacher's direct instruction. There were at least four classes observed
where the discovery of new material was the objective of the
group work.

We found a great diversity in the structuring of groups;
everything from "choose a partner" to groupings that included
students from the top, middle, and lower third of the class in
each group. Teacher-assigned and randomly selected groups
were more frequently on-task than were self-selected groups.
In self-selected groups, students tended to pick friends as
group members, and more socializing seemed to take place.
Given this tendency, it seems that teachers organize groups in
ways other than self-selection so as to maximize task-oriented
interactions.

One problem observed with teacher-organized groups was
students' initial reluctance to work with other students who
were unknown to them. In some classes, teachers created
structures in response to this reluctance. For example, in a biology class the teacher assigned students to work with many
different partners so all students would become acquainted
with the other members of the class and, thus, work more effectively with all of their peers.

In some classes, teachers carefully organized and monitored students' use of time during group work. In classes
where a time limit, stated at the start of an activity, was used to
provide a boundary for group work, students tended to be

more on-task during their allotted work time. Teachers who monitored group progress were able to extend or shorten time limits as student accomplishment demanded or allowed.

Teachers who provided students with specific instructions and group roles also helped them to use group time productively. In both journalism and social studies classes, teachers gave specific instructions for the activities as well as time limits. In a precalculus class, the teacher gave each group member a formal role (e.g., recorder, leader), and these roles helped each group in the class complete its task on time.

We found that teachers used groups as often as daily and as infrequently as once a month. In some classes, such as journalism and biology where students were producing a product or completing labs, the students engage in group work daily.

The diverse kinds of group activities included the following:

- answering a set of teacher-generated questions (English, social studies)
- preparing for a group presentation (English)
- applying a math formula to a new set of circumstances (precalculus)
- brainstorming (*Annual*, world languages)
- problem solving (journalism, biology)
- presenting the answers to last night's homework (geometry)
- paired work to prepare and practice dialogue (world languages)

At Decatur, we observed teachers in all disciplines using group work. We were not invited into every class in the building and were specifically asked not to visit some classes, so we cannot make any observation on the percentage of teachers within the building who actually do use group work in their classroom. But the results of our initial teacher survey indicated that most of our teachers use group work within their curriculum.

## TEACHER INTERVIEWS

### QUESTION 3: WHY DO YOU USE GROUP WORK IN BLOCK PERIODS?

Although it was often given as a "tongue in cheek" response, many teachers stated that they used group work "to survive." It is impossible to maintain student interest in a teacher-directed activity such as lecture for an entire 100-minute period.

A student teacher in Foods noted that groups were the easiest way for her to teach, since she had had considerable instruction in cooperative learning in her preservice preparation. Although the *Annual* teacher had not had extensive training in cooperative learning, she explained that she used groups because the students who know a particular skill will teach it to those who do not and by the end of the semester all students have developed the necessary skills.

### QUESTION 4: AT WHAT POINT IN YOUR LESSON DO YOU USE GROUPS?

Most teachers use groups as part of the process of presenting or exploring new material.

### QUESTION 5: HOW DO YOU EVALUATE GROUP WORK?

In journalism and *Annual* classes, the final product is the published document, which is evaluated using professional publication standards. In world languages, it is the performance of the dialogue for which students are evaluated. Evaluation is based on fluency, pronunciation, and completeness. In Foods, the teacher requires an "exit ticket" in which the students must correctly answer a question based on that day's activities. In biology and mathematics, students turn in a single worksheet that represents the group's work, and each group member receives the grade earned for that worksheet.

Most evaluation of group work is conducted by assessing the quality of a product created by the group members as they work together. One problem raised by this practice is parental objections to a group grade. Some parents see education as a competitive process, not a cooperative one. They do not want their child's grade lowered by the actions of other students. In contrast, many teachers believe that a significant element of group work is for students to learn to collaborate, because collaboration is an essential skill in today's workplace.

### QUESTION 6: DO YOU HAVE TRAINING IN HOW TO USE GROUPS IN YOUR CURRICULUM?

It can be assumed from the questions asked of the teachers who were later observed that 90 percent of them felt that they would benefit from additional training in using groups within the classroom. One of the math teachers observed has given in-service presentations about her application of cooperative learning practices in her classroom.

## STUDENT QUESTIONNAIRE

Responses on the student survey indicate that students do engage in group work in their classes on a regular basis, with almost all responses either at *almost always, sometimes,* or *occasionally.* The responses also support the implicit hypothesis in the questionnaire that teachers use groups to engage students in discussion, definition, gathering information, analysis, and review.

Responses to Question 5 demonstrate that most students have been engaged by their teachers in a discussion focused on the purposes of group work both in the present, in school, and in the future, in the workplace.

Responses to Questions 6 and 8 indicate that the majority of students view themselves as effective group members at least much of the time, and they see groups as effective contexts for academic work and learning.

Responses to Question 7 suggest that the identification and discussion of different group roles vary considerably from one class to the next. On the whole, such identification seems to take place only *sometimes.*

Finally, responses to Questions 6 through 8, compared to responses to previous questions, suggest that students understand the mechanics of group work better than the purposes for which group work is assigned.

One possible problem with several of the questions is that students may not have understood all of the terms, for example, *analyze* or *critique*, in similar ways. Mention of the workplace in Question 5 may also have confused or limited student response to this question.

## ACTION PLAN

Our action plan includes encouraging the administration to provide both additional training in cooperative learning for all faculty members and mentors for new teachers coming into the building who have not previously taught in a block-period environment. We also realized as a research team that we gained ideas from our peers and would like the opportunity to engage in further collaborative action research. We individually gained a greater appreciation for each other on the team and for our fellow teachers.

Additional questions we think could be explored are these:

- ♦ Has there been improvement in student learning with the adoption of 100-minute periods?
- ♦ Are there other refinements to the block-period day that could be made?
- ♦ What additional teaching strategies are being employed by Decatur teachers, and how can they be shared among teachers?

(Ms. Heslop teaches English and accounting. Mr. Hiser teaches German, biology, and special education. Ms. Reed teaches French and German. Mr. Marquez teaches industrial arts.)

## CRITICAL COMMENTS

Jen O'Roarty, who teaches at Renton High School in Renton, Washington, and Bruce Patt, who teaches at Foster High School in Tukwila, Washington, wrote most of the following comments. David Marshak added several elements to this commentary.

### FIRST THOUGHTS

Our first reflection on this report is that there seemed to be a discrepancy in the motivation for restructuring the school's scheduling. The administrators wanted to reduce the amount of tension among students that was a result of the increasingly mobile and ethnically diverse population. The teachers saw this as an opportunity to increase the amount of learning within their classrooms. Because the motivations for restructuring were not consistent, the teachers seemed to find themselves under-prepared as to how they would restructure their teaching and curriculum. Our belief is that a more focused, collaborative vision belonging to both the administrators and teachers would have resulted in a smoother transition from the traditional high school schedule to the new 100-minute block schedule.

Given the perceived incongruity between administrative needs and curricular goals (decreasing student contact time in the halls vs. teaching collaborative "real world" skills), the teachers surveyed seemed to be making some thoughtful and logical adaptations to the situation. This organic movement toward more and more "group work" seemed to us to be the most logical response to the block-period structure. Indeed, the researchers report that every teacher observed (17 teachers of a faculty of 52) employed small groups. The intensive use of small groups is an element identified in Chapter 1 as part of a new model of high school. What we can't discern from this research is *how intensive* the use of groups is at Decatur.

The Decatur researchers also provide a number of specific insights and guidelines about how to organize and structure student work groups so they will be productive and harmonious. These insights and guidelines are of great value to teachers who wish to use small groups effectively.

We congratulate the Decatur teachers for their increased use of groups as this structure also encourages another, in our estimation, "real world" skill: student-directed learning. Working in small groups demands that students become more self-directed as the teacher is not the center of learning. As the study explains, the "discovery of new material" became the curricular goal for more and more teachers as a result of this structure. We found this to be another benefit that deserved more consideration on the part of the research team.

## SOME QUESTIONS

On a related note, we wondered about developing a working definition of the term *group work*. From our perusal of the classroom observation summaries, it seemed that only one of the teachers observed had a clear concept of balancing a degree of individual accountability with group accountability within the construct of what was construed as group work. We felt that it was extremely beneficial that this teacher was able to offer her insights and observations to the entire teaching staff. This is, in our estimation, a vivid example of what the teachers stated they sorely needed—more chances to share with their colleagues in order to realize a more fruitful learning environment for themselves and, consequently, for their students. Still, this begged the question as to what this creature called *group work* looked like. We would have appreciated a clearer definition of what the researchers meant by *group work*. We think that doing so would have focused some of their research and would have provided a common platform for future readers of this study.

Because the focus for restructuring the schedule at Decatur High School was fuzzy, some of the other elements of collaboration were lost on various levels. It seems teachers at Decatur are beginning to recognize the value of a collaborative climate, but have been frustrated by the lack of opportunities afforded them to engage in collegial collaboration. By rethinking the structure of the school, which would have to be spurred on by the administration, more collaboration in teaching strategies would ultimately connect the teachers and classes. Students would be directly impacted because of the potential for more effective teaching strategies within each discipline as well as across disciplines.

## OUR ASSESSMENT

The notion of collegiality and collaboration must be modeled at the highest levels. We saw little evidence that that was the case. We would encourage that. If, in fact, all parties involved believe these to be essential "real world" skills, these skills and values must be modeled at the deepest levels of the school structure. Specifically we would look at three distinct areas:

- ◆ Collaboration among administration, teachers, and support staff for a common vision. To reiterate, our perception is that there exists a discontinuity between the curricular goals of 100-minute periods and the schoolwide goal of reduced student tensions.

- ◆ Integrated curriculum. As mentioned earlier, this must be spurred on by the administration. The administration must make it feasible and desirable by providing release time or common planning periods for teachers to collaborate.

- ◆ Develop a clear definition of *group work* and tie it into specific curricular goals. This should strive to strike a balance between individual student accountability and the success of the entire group.

## FINAL THOUGHTS AND QUESTIONS

First, the decisions made by the administrative team were intended for the benefit of the students. However, the problem that we saw was that beyond making the grand decision to change the scheduling, the administrators did not offer the teachers sufficient professional development to make the transition easier. The tools that many teachers came up with, such as group work, were mentioned as being survival skills as opposed to thought-out teaching practices. The positive feelings that many teachers had about how group work was used in the classroom seemed to be as a result of trial and error as well as retrospective analysis. The evidence that observers were not welcome in some classrooms leads us to believe that with in-service training and better communication among staff members, this defensive posture would not have been as prevalent.

Second, the report, unfortunately, does not provide data that correlates the frequency of small-group usage with the implementation of a block-period schedule. It seems reasonable, however, to assume that the use of small groups has increased in the block-period schedule in light of the following comment offered by the researchers: "Although it was often given as a 'tongue in cheek' response, many teachers stated that they used group work 'to survive.' It is impossible to maintain student interest in a teacher-directed activity such as lecture for an entire 100-minute period." The fact that teachers explain that they use group work "to survive" rather than in recognition of its powerful value as pedagogy suggests that some or many teachers in the school are still operating largely from the conventional model of high school, even within a block-period schedule. A later observation by the researchers also supports this hypothesis: "Finally, responses to Questions 6 through 8 (in the student survey), compared to responses to previous questions, suggest that students understand the mechanics of group work better than the purposes for which group work is assigned." Teaching students the *how* without addressing the *why* is a recurring element of the conventional approach to high school.

If many or most teachers are operating from the conventional model, it raises questions about the premise articulated in Chapter 1 about the nature of block periods as change agents: "The block period of 80 minutes or more is a slow-acting poison in the bloodstream of the conventional paradigm of high school. Slowly but surely, the block period challenges the continued function of 40–50-minute classes and all of the assumptions and values embedded within them." Perhaps not. Perhaps teachers can move into a block-period structure and maintain most of the assumptions and values of the conventional paradigm. And if so, can they do this indefinitely?

Third, the researchers note:

> Most evaluation of group work is conducted by assessing the quality of a product created by the group members as they work together. One problem raised by this practice is parental objections to a group grade. Some parents see education as a competitive process, not a cooperative one. They do not want their child's grade lowered by the actions of other students. In contrast, many teachers believe that a significant element of group work is for students to learn to collaborate, because collaboration is an essential skill in today's workplace.

This observation identifies an important issue, which in some ways can be understood as a conflict between the conventional model of high school and which is largely individualistic and competitive, and the new model, which is individualistic and competitive at times *and* collaborative and collegial at other times.

Finally, in the end, what impressed us most about this study and the people involved in it was what we viewed as a very honest, open, and sincere questioning and evaluation of their own professional practice. We admired this as it heartened us, as beginners in this profession, to see people actively involved with improving their own teaching and doing this with a larger goal in mind—providing a quality and meaningful education to the students that they serve. This type of openness needs to be encouraged and applauded within the teaching community.

## APPENDIX 7.1. FACULTY SURVEY

Faculty Survey
  to be used to determine CAR
question

Subject matter taught _____

1. Please list and describe briefly
three classroom teaching strategies
that you are using sucessfully in
your 100 minute class periods.

1.


2.


3.


Please list and describe one thing
that you would change in our current
altered day schedule.

## APPENDIX 7.2. TEACHER INTERVIEW QUESTIONS

INSTRUCTIONS TO THE INTERVIWER:  Please ask the teacher the following questions.  Try not to elaborate or lead the teacher into a response.  Every interview should be as consistent as possible. Be sure to have a cassette tape recording as back-up.

SUBJECT AREA:                    GRADE LEVEL:

1.  How do you structure groups?
    a)   Do students have specific roles assigned within the
         group?

    b)   Are the groups collaborative in nature?

2.  How often do you use groups?

3.  Why do you use group work as an instructional strategy in extended periods?

4.  At what point in your lesson do you use groups?  (discovery, introduction, application, evaluation)

5.  How do you evaluate group work?
    a)   How do you evaluate student performance?

    b)   How do you evaluate the success of the activity for the
         intended outcome?

6.  Do you have training in how to use groups in your curriculum?
    a)   If so, please describe.  How has it impacted what you do?
    b)   If not, what kind of training would facilitate what
         you need?

---
**APPENDIX 7.3. CLASSROOM OBSERVATION FORM**
---

*Name of class being observed* _____

*Date and time of observation* _____

*Specific lesson material being covered by the instructor :*

*What percentage of the class time was used for group work?*

*What instructions were given to the student before the group work began?*


*Specific group observations :*

    *What size were the groups?*

    *Were groups self chosen or were they teacher assigned?*

    *Were specific tasks, i.e. facilitator, time-keeper, etc. assigned to group members?*

    *Did the groups have a sense of purpose?*

    *Was the entire group membership engaged?*

    *What percentage of students in the group participated in the task at hand?*

    *How was the participation measured?*

    *Did groups have an ongoing project or one that was completed during that class period?*

## APPENDIX 7.4. STUDENT EVALUATION OF GROUP WORK

Group work based on a mutual concern for the needs of students in an extended period of a modified school day.

Directions: Evaluate group work in this classroom using the scale below and circle the appropriate number to indicate how group work was used.

1    Always
2    Almost Always
3    Sometimes
4    Occasionally
5    Never

1. We use small group settings to discuss and define concepts.
     1     2     3     4     5

2. We use small groups to gather and analyze information.
     1     2     3     4     5

3. We use small group settings to review topics.
     1     2     3     4     5

4. We use small groups to critique oral and written reports.
     1     2     3     4     5

5. We have discussed the use of small group activities in the classroom and the work place.
     1     2     3     4     5

6. We work effectively as a group toward the completion of projects or products.
     1     2     3     4     5

7. We have identified roles that occur in small group structures.
     1     2     3     4     5

8. I contribute effectively to the group outcomes in various roles.
     1     2     3     4     5

## APPENDIX 7.5. FACULTY RESPONSES

CLASSROOM STRATEGIES FOR ESL
1. 10 minute journal
2. 20 minute grammar review worksheets or workbook
3. Remainder of class is for reading and literature

CLASSROOM STRATEGIES FOR ENGLISH
1. Variety
2. Review before test
3. More discussion time

1. Journals
2. L.A.P. work
3. Projects

1. Small group work
2. Teaching a complete lesson
3. Reading then responses.

1. Variety
2. Group projects
3. Games

1. Group work
2. Individual research
3. Group research

1. Combination of lecture and demonstration
2. Length of class
3. Longer work time

1. Group work
2. Lecture and demonstration
3. Work due at end of class
1. Reading time
2. Writing LAB
3. Discussions

1. Field trips
2. Games
3. Group work

FOREIGN LANGUAGES
1. Oral communication
2. Writing activities

1. Lots questions
2. Group activities
3. Student dialogues

1. Multiple activities
2. Individual help (more)
3. Hands on projects

```
SCHOOL 4
1. Lecture
2. Discussion
3. Tapes and videos
4. Cooperative learning

SCIENCE/BIOLOGY
1. Numerous activities
2. Station activities
3. More time

1. Lecture
2. Questions and book reading
3. Fit subject matter

1. Period devoted to one topic
2. Student prep and projects

1. Variety
2. Incorporate cooperative learning
3. Plan ahead

1. Doing warm-ups
2. More labs
3. Never give lecture for more than 20min

1. Use several activities
2. Give breaks
3. Individual instruction as well as other

HISTORY
1. Smaller activities
2. Applying skills with videos
3. Students help other students

1. Current news sessions
2. Exercises with assignments
3. Group assignments

1. Variety
2. Lesson plan block
3. Hands on

MATH
1. More discipline
2. Review possibilities around test taking
3. Practice test

1. Lecture work/Lecture work
2. Study in groups
3. Give study time
```

1. Warm-ups at beginning of each period
2. Frequent change of activities
3. Breaks during class

1. Breaking activities into thirds
2. Have time to put up problems on board
3. Time to do short video presentations

CONSUMER & FAMILY SCIENCES
1. Present information
2. Field trips
3. Extended time for proper food preparation

1. Small group work
2. Team projects
3. Hands on experiences

BUSINESS
1. Don't lecture for a full 100 minute
2. Hands on application
3. Great use for speakers

1. Change activities frequently
2. Increase hands-on

SPECIAL VOCATIONAL DEV.
1. Some fun activities
2. Have several short activities
3. Keep their attention span

MARKETING
1. Teacher time/student time
2. Application time
3. Modified instruction

1. Lecture
2. Small group projects
3. Specialized instruction

Physical education

1. Students teaching certain skills
2. Develop skill level from each student

COUNSELING 9
1. ?

ANNUAL ART
1. Show slides with a lecture
2. Alot more time to accomplish things
3. Group activities

PHOTOGRAPHY/POTTERY
1. Combination of lecture and demonstration
2. Good studio time

# 8

# LINDBERGH HIGH SCHOOL
## TECHNOLOGY IN BLOCK PERIODS

Helen Bedtelyon, Chris Drape
Jef Rettmann, Jeannie Wenndorf

## SCHOOL PORTRAIT AND INTRODUCTION

Lindbergh High School enrolls just over 1,200 students in grades 9 through 12. The school is located in Renton, Washington, a first-ring suburb to the southeast of Seattle. Thirty-two percent of the students at Lindbergh are persons of color.

In 1992, the Renton School District passed a $17 million technology levy that allowed the district to become one of the most technologically advanced districts in the state. At Lindbergh High School, each room in the building is connected to the rest of the district via a computer network. Also, each classroom has at least two computers with direct access to the Internet. The main computer lab has 57 Power Macintosh computers, each of which is also connected to the network. There are also two minilabs, one with 14 Macintosh computers and the other with 30. The building has a variety of other technologies available to faculty and students, such as scanners, digital cameras, and PC viewers.

At the beginning of the 1995–96 school year, Lindbergh High School switched from the traditional six-period day to a three-period day. In the new schedule, Mondays are standard six-period days, while the rest of the days of the week have three 105-minute periods. Periods 1, 3, and 5 meet on Tuesdays and Thursdays, and periods 2, 4, and 6 meet on Wednesdays and Fridays. There is a 20-minute *advisory period* that meets Tuesday through Friday.

The decision to change to a block-period schedule began in 1993, when the staff at Lindbergh High School received a grant from the Renton School District to explore site-based decision-making. With this grant, the faculty formed what was called the Learning Improvement Team (LIT). LIT coordinated a faculty-wide discussion on the state of the school. During the 1994–95 school year, smaller teams of faculty members were formed to examine specific areas of need. Two main goals were developed as a result of the efforts of these teams: (1) to improve the climate for student learning, and (2) to foster an environment that allows teachers to develop relationships that are more meaningful with students.

Once these two goals were identified and agreed upon by the faculty, the LIT team worked on a proposal that would allow Lindbergh to achieve them. Team members examined other schools and other school models that addressed these goals. LIT came to the conclusion that reconfiguring the time schedule was the best way to meet these goals. They then presented their proposal to change to the three-period day to the rest of the faculty in the spring of 1995. Eighty-five percent of the 52-member faculty voted in favor of the change.

During the spring of 1996, at the end of the first year with the block-period schedule, the students and staff at Lindbergh High School overwhelmingly voted to continue with the three-period day. Both students and staff felt that the new schedule slowed the day down, making it less hectic and rushed. Students felt that the long periods allowed for more teacher–student one-on-one interaction, giving students more opportunities to get help on assignments from their teachers. Students also liked only having three classes to focus on each night in terms of homework. Teachers felt that the long periods allowed them to do labs and in-class projects that they could not do within the 55-minute periods.

In spite of the high degree of support for continuing the three-period day, there are a few issues and concerns that need to be addressed further. The music and foreign language departments feel that the decrease in the number of days that the teachers see the students, from 5 days with the six-period day down to 3 days with the block-period schedule, hurts student learning in the classes taught in those departments. This has led to a conflict concerning our Monday schedule. The majority of the teachers would like to eliminate the six-period Monday in order to go to a three-period day schedule each day of the week. The staff narrowly voted to keep the six-period Monday schedule, however, in order to accommodate the concerns of the music and foreign language departments.

A second concern among the faculty about the three-period day is the creation of the *advisory period*. Some faculty members want to eliminate *advisory*, some want to keep it but make changes in how it is run, and some want to keep it as is. The faculty voted to keep the *advisory period*, but to make some changes that essentially give students more freedom in how they use this time.

The third issue regarding the block period deals with the changes in pedagogical strategy necessitated by the longer periods. Many teachers have felt they have had to learn new strategies in order to teach effectively with the new schedule. This is an area where an ongoing dialogue among the faculty needs to take place, and it is in this area that we focused our research efforts.

## RESEARCH METHODOLOGY

Our process of formulating a research question was fairly straightforward. All four members of our research team had an interest in exploring effective methods of engaging students during the block period, and we wanted to focus on something that we could manageably study given the constraints of our research. The 1992 technology levy provided us with a substantial resource base of computers and software. This year our school went "online," getting connected to the Internet and e-mail. Given these factors, the effective use of technology was an important issue for our building, so we decided to combine the two ideas, computer-based technology and block periods, as the heart of our inquiry.

We next established six assumptions in our research problem statement:

- With the block-period day, it is essential that students be actively engaged in the learning process.
- Teachers need more tools and methods to enhance student engagement in the block periods.
- Technology can be used as one tool to engage students actively in the learning process.
- Our school currently has a large amount of technology available that is being underused by teachers and students.
- This lack of use of technology stems from a lack of technological literacy on the part of teachers, a lack of time to gain computer literacy and skills, and a lack of time to plan lessons that integrate technology in the classroom.
- The block-period day should allow for increased use of technology in the teaching–learning process.

Our research question then emerged: *How can the block period allow for an increased use of technology to engage students more actively in the learning process?*

This question led to two more questions:

- What kinds of effective, engaging activities are possible with technology?
- What keeps teachers from using technology more often and more effectively?

We then developed and enacted the three components of our research process:

*A Faculty Survey (see Appendix 8.1):* This survey was given to the entire faculty (52 faculty members; 30 surveys returned). The survey focused on teacher use of technology, changes in use due to our move to a block-period schedule, and teacher perception of technology's effectiveness in block periods.

*An "Expert" Interview (see Appendix 8.2):* We identified four faculty members who we deemed technology experts for our building based on their knowledge and previous use of technology in the classroom. The interviews were designed to elicit specific information about how these teachers have made technology an effective method for block-period teaching, as well as why they believe it is effective.

*A Student Survey (see Appendix 8.3):* We administered a student survey to 82 students in four different advisory classes. The purpose of the student surveys was to measure student perception of technology use and effectiveness. Did students think technology was a meaningful learning tool in block periods? How often were they using technology and for what purpose? We wanted to be able to compare student perceptions with faculty perceptions to gauge whether both groups agreed on technology's effectiveness.

We had originally planned a second component to the expert interview, interviewing identified "experts" outside our building. We planned to use these interviews to explore more directly the specific types and uses of technology that work well in block periods, including what makes these types especially effective. We chose not to pursue this for two reasons: lack of response from the experts we contacted and the realization that the scope of our research was not large enough to analyze the individual effectiveness of different types of technology adequately. We decided to focus instead on what was happening in our building with technology and how that is related to the block period. The effectiveness of particular technologies can be the subject of future study.

## FINDINGS AND ANALYSIS

There were a number of important conclusions that resulted from our research. These findings are not surprising, but
they do confirm our assumptions going into the research.

- A variety of activities that encourage student
  engagement are a necessary component of effective teaching in block-period classes.
- Using technology well in the high school classroom requires large amounts of time, which a
  block-period schedule provides.
- Students like using technology.
- Most teachers like using technology.
- Students believe that using technology makes
  class more interesting and helps them to learn
  more.
- Teachers believe that using technology in class is
  an effective use of time in terms of student
  learning.
- Teachers believe that the block-period schedule
  increases the opportunities for using technology
  in class.
- The lack of time for planning and training keeps
  many teachers from using technology more often and more effectively.
- The majority of technology use occurred in
  teacher preparation for classes, not in "hands-
  on" student activities.

From the teachers' perspectives, technology is a useful tool
for engaging students. The experts we interviewed spoke of a
need for a variety of activities within the block period, and
technology was a key component in this variety. Perhaps our
most significant finding from the teachers' experience, however, was the fact that majority of teacher use of technology
takes place in preparation time, not student use time. This illustrates an important fact about technology in the classrooms:

Teacher comfort and familiarity with technology is necessary to infuse technology use into students' activities in the classroom.

From both the surveys and the interviews, it became clear that time is a key factor in the effective use of technology. Not only are blocks of time necessary for effective use of technology with students, but time is also needed for teachers to become knowledgeable enough with various and new types of technology to allow the move from personal use in preparation to student-centered use in the classroom. The bottom line is that technology is an effective way to engage students in block periods, but that teachers need training and planning time to make better use of technology in the classroom.

From the student surveys, it was clear that there is an interest in and affinity for computer-based technology, both important factors for student engagement. The student survey supports the notion that students find technology effective for their own learning. Students also note that there is room for an increase in the amount of technology employed in the classroom. These findings confirmed assumptions we made before we began our study, namely that technology can be an effective tool in the classroom but that we have room to grow in terms of its use and application.

Because we added new technology options this school year (i.e., Internet capabilities, in-district e-mail), we could not isolate the impact that our move to block periods had on teacher technology use, but the following statistics describe some connections between block periods and technology use. (See Appendix 8.4 for a complete summary of the faculty survey results and Appendix 8.5 for the student survey results.)

## SELECTED FACULTY SURVEY AND INTERVIEW RESULTS

Survey Questions 4 and 5 gauged teacher technology use before and after our move to block periods. There were increases in all categories of technology use.

Survey Question 6 gauged the reasons for this increased use of technology:

♦ 26 percent of the faculty said BLOCK PERIODS contributed to the increase.

♦ 60 percent of the faculty said NEW KNOWL-EDGE contributed to the increase.

♦ 70 percent of the faculty said the availability of NEW TECHNOLOGY contributed to the increase.

In survey Question 10, 70 percent of the teachers said block periods allowed for greater use of technology.

In survey Question 9, 50 percent of the teachers said LACK OF PLANNING TIME was the primary factor that kept them from using technology more.

In survey Question 9, 23 percent of the faculty said LACK OF KNOWLEDGE was the primary factor that kept them from using technology more.

In survey Question 11, 63 percent of the teachers reported TEACHER PREPARATION as their primary use of technology.

## SELECTED STUDENT SURVEY RESULTS

In Question 1, 82 percent of students surveyed said they liked using technology.

In Question 3, 67 percent of students surveyed said using technology helped them learn better.

In Question 4, 62 percent of students surveyed said using technology made class more interesting and engaging.

Survey Question 5 asked students to rank the amount that teachers incorporate technology into class:

A lot: 10%
Some: 52%
Not much: 34%
Not at all: 4%

## CONCLUSION

It is significant that all 30 of the teachers responded that they would participate in technology training if it were made available (faculty survey Question 13). The teachers desire to learn more about technology. Given the technology resources that our building has, some of which are currently underutilized, it is to our advantage to provide focused professional development that will help teachers make the transition from the personal use of technology to instructional uses in the classroom. For those of us doing the research, this entire process has motivated us to make better use of what we have available. It has been an encouragement for us to recognize the importance of challenging ourselves in the kind of learning activities that we attempt with students in the classroom.

These findings give us insight into the second part of our research question: *What keeps teachers from using technology more?* But we only touched upon the first part of the question: *What kinds of effective, engaging activities are possible with technology?* Future study would be helpful into what specific forms of technology are especially engaging and useful in the block period and how these forms can be employed.

The block-period schedule provides unique challenges for student engagement. As the technology available to teachers continues to grow, it is increasingly important that we thoughtfully explore the effective use of technology in the classroom as a teaching tool that actively engages students in the learning process.

(Ms. Bedtelyon and Mr. Rettman teach language arts. Mr. Drape teaches social studies. Ms. Wenndorf teaches biology.)

## CRITICAL COMMENTS

Christine Corbley and Paul Harvey wrote most of the following comments. They teach at Highline High School, which serves several communities just south of Seattle, including Burien, White Center, and Des Moines. David Marshak added several elements to this commentary.

## THE RESEARCH PROCESS

The motivation for the two surveys and a set of interviews was sound and relevant. It was important to gather information from people who would be most affected by the modified schedule and the introduction of technology, that is, the teachers and students. A few concerns appeared, however, as we reviewed the content of the questionnaires in light of the original question. The surveys asked many questions that addressed how technology was being used at Lindbergh. These questions are relevant insofar as they lead to an assessment of whether these uses are effective in engaging students. The research question appears to ask how technology can be used in a block period relative to student engagement. A few of the questions appeared to be more concerned with perceptions of technology (Questions 1 and 2) than with its use and effect on engagement. This aspect of the surveys made it unclear whether the surveys were attempting to assess Lindbergh's current system or were looking for methods to improve student engagement. There were several questions that were quite relevant and that should have been the main focus of the research. On the faculty surveys, Questions 4, 5, 6, 7, 9, and 11 were particularly relevant. Question 10 was very well designed in that it dealt with the connections between block periods and the use of technology. A good follow-up question would have been this: "How has the use of technology affected student engagement?" The best research questions came in the form of Questions 1, 3, and 4 in the expert survey. These questions were directly relevant to the research question and should have been asked in all surveys.

It was admirable that the survey was directed toward those who would be most affected. It was also wise to solicit information from experts. A few questions came up as we examined this. First, was there an attempt to seek out expert information from *students* who had experience with technology? This may have been a valuable resource in that it may have provided insight into not only how to engage students more actively, but also how students who are technologically literate perceive engagement, the uses of technology, and the extended period.

It appears that greater effort could have been made to gain information from outside experts. It is understandable that some people are poor in responding to solicitations for information. Other resources, however, could have been tapped that were absent from this research. These resources include literature such as educational journal publications and books about the three subjects, professors of educational technology at the university level, and curriculum specialists from other districts that have both technological resources and block-period schedules.

Another concern is the perceived low level of response of staff in the survey results. What were the reasons for this low level of response? How might a greater percentage of staff been motivated to respond?

Generally, the research process aimed at gathering information related to the question. More specific questioning about how the three variables interrelate and a broader base of resources may have helped yield more data. A broader use of expert interview questions would also have helped.

## CRITIQUE OF THE FINDINGS

To use technology effectively, it is important to have block periods. The time allows teachers and students to use the technology more effectively, and the staff and students appreciate the extended time. The finding of student and staff enjoyment is more an expression of perceptions than a response to the questions of how to use block periods effectively. The findings of the research are interesting, but they do not really answer the research question: *How can the block period allow for increased use of technology to engage students more actively in the learning process?*

The Lindbergh researchers found a need for training and more planning time, but how does that finding relate to the block period? They did find that teachers use technology more in block periods, and this is a worthwhile and useful finding.

However, they could have gathered more specific data about how teachers had increased their use of technology in block periods in comparison with short periods. The researchers found that their faculty has room to grow in its use of technology and that they need to focus on the application of technology in the classroom. We would have liked to see a plan of action based on their findings.

With teachers and students more active within block periods, there is greater opportunity for the use of technology. We are still unclear as to the "how" dimension. How best can teachers use these technologies in block periods? There is also a need for a variety of activities and training, but the survey is not specific enough to identify what those activities should be or what training is needed. The researchers also should have given the expert interview to everyone as part of their interviewing process, because it includes several key questions that get to the heart of their inquiry.

## CRITIQUE OF ANALYSIS AND DISCUSSION

The analysis and critique seems a bit superficial in its content. It is not really focused on the findings and seems to be based on the researchers' impressions rather than on their research. Their findings are expected, and there are no surprises, as the researchers note. What seems to be missing is a discussion of the possibilities related to their findings. How can this technology be used in block periods?

## A FEW LAST THOUGHTS

The findings of the Lindbergh study identify three elements that suggest steps toward a new model of high school: teachers' perceptions of the need to employ a "variety of activities that encourage student engagement" in block periods; teachers' beliefs that "the block-period schedule increases the opportunities for using technology in class"; and an acknowledgment by teachers of the need for ongoing exploration and experimentation, in this case with a focus on the teaching and learning uses of new technologies, particularly computer-related ones.

The researchers note that "using technology well in the high school classroom requires large amounts of time, which a block-period schedule provides." As the Internet and the World Wide Web increasingly become the locus of activity for research and communication, the need for time grows, because, at least at present, access and maneuverability on the Web are variable. Many Web-based activities just cannot be done in 20 or 30 minutes.

The finding from the student reports that 82 percent of students surveyed said they liked using technology, 67 percent of students surveyed said using technology helped them learn better, and 62 percent of students surveyed said using technology made class more interesting and engaging is striking. It confirms, as the researchers note, that "there is an interest in and affinity for computer-based technology, both important factors for student engagement." It would be interesting to see the student responses disaggregated in terms of gender, family income, ethnicity, and age.

The researchers' finding that "the majority of technology use occurred in teacher preparation for classes, not in 'hands-on' student activities" is telling. It informs us that in this school, at least, and probably in many others, there is a significant gap between the availability of computer hardware and software and teachers' development of skills for using these tools for teaching and learning in the classroom. One hypothesis about this gap is that without block periods, teachers will have less motivation to close the gap. Why learn a set of new teaching skills if you never have time to employ them in your classroom?

## APPENDIX 8.1. FACULTY SURVEY

### TECHNOLOGY USE IN EXTENDED PERIODS

The following survey is part of a research project on the extended period day. We are part of a research consortium (including Seattle University and 9 other area high schools) working to expand the knowledge base regarding effective teaching and learning in extended periods. We have chosen to look into the effectiveness of technology as a teaching tool in extended periods, and the following survey will serve as a starting point in gauging Lindbergh faculty's general knowledge and use. The surveys are anonymous, but please fill in your department above.
We appreciate your time on this. THANKS!
   Helen, Chris, Duane, Jef, Jeannie

1. Indicate your comfort level with technology (see list of examples in question 3).
   ___ very comfortable ___ comfortable ___ somewhat comfortable ___ not comfortable

2. Indicate the level of availability of technology we have in our building.
   ___ very available ___ somewhat available      ___ not available

3. Rank your competency level for each of the following. (1 = "very competent" 2 = "somewhat competent" 3 = "no knowledge of")
   ___ word processor        ___ CD-ROM         ___ PC-Viewer
   ___ scanner               ___ e-mail         ___ computer simulations
   ___ Internet              ___ t.v./VCR       ___ other: _____

4. What types of technology did you use with your classes BEFORE we changed to the three-period day? (check all that apply)
   ___ word processor        ___ CD-ROM         ___ PC-Viewer
   ___ scanner               ___ e-mail         ___ computer simulations
   ___ Internet              ___ t.v./VCR       ___ other: _____

5. What types of technology have you used THIS YEAR? (check all that apply)
   ___ word processor        ___ CD-ROM         ___ PC-Viewer
   ___ scanner               ___ e-mail         ___ computer simulations
   ___ Internet              ___ t.v./VCR       ___ other: _____

6. If there has been a change in your technology use, to what is this due? (check all that apply)
   ___ extended periods
   ___ new knowledge on your part
   ___ new technology available in the building
   ___ other: _____

7. Indicate the frequency of classroom use for the following types of technology. (1 = daily, 2 = 2-3 times/week, 3 = once a week, 4 = monthly, 5 = less than once a month, 6 = never)
___ word processor ___ CD-ROM ___ PC-Viewer
___ scanner ___ e-mail ___ computer simulations
___ Internet ___ t.v./VCR ___ other: _____

8. Which types of technology would you like to use that you currently do not? (check all...)
___ word processor ___ CD-ROM ___ PC-Viewer
___ scanner ___ e-mail ___ computer simulations
___ Internet ___ t.v./VCR ___ other: _____

9. What keeps you from using technology more than you currently do. (Rank all that apply, with "1" being the most important reason)
___ lack of knowledge
___ lack of planning time
___ lack of availability to needed technology
___ lack of perceived need to use technology
___ other: _____

10. To what degree do the extended periods allow you to make greater use of technology with your students?
___ much more ___ a little more ___ no more ___ less

11. How is technology used with your classes? (Rank: 1 = most common ... 6 = least common)
___ student research
___ student word processing
___ student projects (simulations, presentations, etc.)
___ teacher preparation/research
___ teacher presentations/demonstrations
___ other: _____

12. Where do your students most often use technology for your class? (Rank: 1 = most use ... 3 = least use)
___ computer lab
___ library
___ classroom

13. If technology training (including ideas for effective/creative use in extended periods) were offered, would you participate?
___ yes
___ no

14. If technology training were made available, how would you like it to be set up? (Rank: 1 = first choice, 5 = last choice)
___ half-day workshop(s)
___ full day inservice
___ after school training
___ Saturday training
___ other: _____

15. Please add any additional comments, questions, or information you think would be helpful:

## APPENDIX 8.2. EXPERT INTERVIEW QUESTIONS

1. What kinds of technology do you use with your students? How often? Describe your favorite/most effective use of technology with students. Why do you think this is especially effective?

2. What experience or training have you had that has helped increase your knowledge and comfort level with technology? What is the most valuable training you've had in terms of using technology with your students? What training would you recommend for teachers interested in using more hands-on, technology-based activities with their students?

3. How engaged do your students seem when you teach hands-on, tech-based activities? How does this compare to their engagement levels when you use more traditional, non-tech-based methods?

4. How have the extended periods changed the way you use technology with your students? What are some specific technology-based activities you have used in extended periods that weren't well-suited to 55-minute periods?

## APPENDIX 8.3. STUDENT TECHNOLOGY SURVEY

**STUDENT TECHNOLOGY SURVEY:** Please answer the following questions. For the purposes of this survey, anything that is electronic could be considered "technology."

1. Do you like using technology?

_____ yes _____ no _____ indifferent

2. Indicate your overall COMFORT LEVEL with technology.

___ very comfortable ___ comfortable ___ not comfortable

3. Does the use of technology in class help you to learn better?

_____ yes _____ no _____ indifferent

4. Does using technology make class more interesting or engaging for you?

_____ yes _____ no _____ indifferent

5. How much do your **TEACHERS** incorporate the use of technology in your classes?

_____ a lot _____ some _____ not much _____ not at all

6. Which of the following types of technology do your **TEACHERS** use to present material and to teach lessons?

| | | |
|---|---|---|
| ____ Word processor | ____ CD-ROM | ____ PC-Viewer (attached to overhead projector) |
| ____ scanner | ____ e-mail | ____ computer simulations |
| ____ internet | ____ t.v./VCR | ____ overhead projector |

7. Which of the following types of technology do YOU use to do projects and assignments for your classes?

| | | |
|---|---|---|
| ____ Word processor | ____ CD-ROM | ____ PC-Viewer (attached to overhead projector) |
| ____ scanner | ____ e-mail | ____ computer simulations |
| ____ internet | ____ t.v./VCR | |

8. How often do YOU use technology for class assignments or projects?

_____ daily _____ weekly _____ monthly _____ not at all

9. Which types of technology would YOU like to use for your class work that you currently do not?

| | | |
|---|---|---|
| ____ Word processor | ____ CD-ROM | ____ PC-Viewer |
| ____ scanner | ____ e-mail | ____ computer simulations |
| ____ internet | ____ t.v./VCR | |

10. Rank the level of AVAILABILITY of the technology we have in our building.

_____ very available _____ somewhat available _____ not available

## APPENDIX 8.4. FACULTY SURVEY RESULTS

The results of our faculty survey follow below. The numbers indicate the number of teachers who responded to each part of each question. Thirty faculty surveys were returned. When numbers do not total thirty it is because some responses were left blank.

1. Indicate your comfort level with technology (see list of examples in question 3).

8____ very comfortable  12____comfortable  7____ somewhat comfortable  1___ not comfortable

2. Indicate the level of availability of technology we have in our building.

11___ very available      16___ somewhat available        0____ not available

3. Rank your competency level for each of the following. (1 = "very competent" 2 = "somewhat competent" 3 = "no knowledge of")

|                      | very competent (1) | somewhat competent (2) | no knowledge of (3) |
|----------------------|--------------------|------------------------|---------------------|
| word processor       | 22                 | 7                      | 1                   |
| scanner              | 2                  | 10                     | 17                  |
| Internet             | 10                 | 18                     | 2                   |
| CD-ROM               | 11                 | 9                      | 9                   |
| e-mail               | 10                 | 18                     | 2                   |
| t.v./VCR             | 28                 | 1                      | 1                   |
| PC-Viewer            | 5                  | 9                      | 14                  |
| computer simulations | 10                 | 7                      | 12                  |
| other                | 5                  | 2                      |                     |

4. What types of technology did you use with your classes BEFORE we changed to the three-period day? (check all that apply)

| 26___ | word processor | 8____ | CD-ROM   | 3____  | PC-Viewer            |
|-------|----------------|-------|----------|--------|----------------------|
| 4____ | scanner        | 5____ | e-mail   | 10____ | computer simulations |
| 5____ | Internet       | 26___ | t.v./VCR | 6____  | other: _____  |

5. What types of technology have you used THIS YEAR? (check all that apply)

| 30___ | word processor | 14___ | CD-ROM   | 6____  | PC-Viewer            |
|-------|----------------|-------|----------|--------|----------------------|
| 8____ | scanner        | 24___ | e-mail   | 12____ | computer simulations |
| 23___ | Internet       | 26___ | t.v./VCR | 7____  | other: _____  |

6. If there has been a change in your technology use, to what is this due? (check all that apply)

8_____ extended periods
18_____ new knowledge on your part
21_____ new technology available in the building
3_____ other: _____

7. Indicate the frequency of classroom use for the following types of technology. (1 = daily, 2 = 2-3 times/week, 3 = once a week, 4 = monthly, 5 = less than once a month, 6 = never)

| | daily | 2-3/week | 1/week | monthly | <1/month | never |
|---|---|---|---|---|---|---|
| word processor | 11 | 7 | 0 | 2 | 6 | 1 |
| scanner | 0 | 2 | 0 | 4 | 3 | 8 |
| Internet | 2 | 6 | 1 | 2 | 8 | 6 |
| CD-ROM | 3 | 2 | 1 | 2 | 4 | 5 |
| e-mail | 10 | 5 | 3 | 0 | 2 | 3 |
| t.v./VCR | 4 | 3 | 7 | 5 | 3 | 1 |
| PC-Viewer | 4 | 0 | 0 | 1 | 1 | 10 |
| computer simulations | 2 | 0 | 0 | 2 | 6 | 7 |
| other | 2 | 1 | 0 | 0 | 2 | 0 |

8. Which types of technology would you like to use that you currently do not? (check all...)

0_____ word processor    12_____ CD-ROM    15_____ PC-Viewer
16_____ scanner    6_____ e-mail    9_____ computer simulations
5_____ Internet    1_____ t.v./VCR    0_____ other: _____

9. What keeps you from using technology more than you currently do. (Rank all that apply, with "1" being the most important reason)

| | 1 | 2 | 3 | 4 | 5 |
|---|---|---|---|---|---|
| lack of knowledge | 7 | 8 | 6 | 1 | 0 |
| lack of planning time | 15 | 5 | 4 | 0 | 0 |
| lack of availability to needed technology | 6 | 6 | 7 | 2 | 0 |
| lack of perceived need to use technology | 3 | 3 | 3 | 6 | 1 |
| other: | 4 | 0 | 0 | 0 | 1 |

10. To what degree do the extended periods allow you to make greater use of technology with your students?

5_____ much more    16_____ a little more   9_____ no more    0_____ less

11. How is technology used with your classes? (Rank: 1 = most common ... 6 = least common)

|                                       | 1  | 2 | 3 | 4 | 5 | 6 |
|---------------------------------------|----|---|---|---|---|---|
| student research                      | 3  | 4 | 8 | 4 | 2 | 3 |
| student word processing               | 7  | 4 | 6 | 1 | 5 | 2 |
| student projects                      | 6  | 6 | 4 | 4 | 1 | 1 |
| teacher preparation/research          | 19 | 3 | 3 | 2 | 0 | 0 |
| teacher presentations/demonstrations 8 | 9 | 5 | 1 | 0 | 1 |   |
| other                                 | 1  | 0 | 0 | 0 | 0 | 0 |

12. Where do your students most often use technology for your class? (Rank: 1 = most use ...  3 = least use)

|               | 1  | 2  | 3  |
|---------------|----|----|----|
| computer lab  | 7  | 14 | 4  |
| library       | 5  | 9  | 9  |
| classroom     | 17 | 1  | 10 |

13. If technology training (including ideas for effective/creative use in extended periods) were offered, would you participate?

<u>30</u>      yes          <u>0</u>      no

14. If technology training were made available, how would you like it to be set up? (Rank: 1 = first choice... 5 = last choice)

|                       | 1  | 2  | 3  | 4  | 5 |
|-----------------------|----|----|----|----|---|
| half-day workshop(s) 24 | 4 | 0  | 0  | 0  |   |
| full day inservice    | 3  | 16 | 5  | 0  | 0 |
| after school training | 2  | 5  | 16 | 2  | 0 |
| Saturday training     | 0  | 2  | 2  | 15 | 3 |

## APPENDIX 8.5. STUDENT SURVEY RESULTS

1. Do you like using technology?

<u>67</u>   yes        <u>2</u>   no        <u>13</u>   indifferent

2. Indicate your overall COMFORT LEVEL with technology.

<u>36</u>   very comfortable        <u>48</u>   comfortable        <u>7</u>   not comfortable

3. Does the use of technology in class help you to learn better?

<u>56</u>   yes        <u>6</u>   no        <u>21</u>   indifferent

4. Does using technology make class more interesting or engaging for you?

<u>54</u>   yes        <u>17</u>   no        <u>16</u>   indifferent

5. How much do your TEACHERS incorporate the use of technology in your classes?

<u>8</u>   a lot        <u>42</u>   some        <u>27</u>   not much        <u>3</u>   not at all

6. Which of the following types of technology do your TEACHERS use to present material and to teach lessons?

<u>31</u> Word processor        <u>24</u>  CD-ROM        <u>27</u>  PC-Viewer (attached to overhead projector) __
<u>7</u> scanner        <u>9</u>  e-mail        <u>25</u>  computer simulations
<u>26</u> internet        <u>62</u>  t.v./VCR        <u>63</u>  overhead projector

7. Which of the following types of technology do YOU use to do projects and assignments for your classes?

<u>56</u> Word processor        <u>31</u>  CD-ROM        <u>8</u>  PC-Viewer (attached to overhead projector) __
<u>5</u> scanner        <u>3</u>  e-mail        <u>19</u>  computer simulations
<u>37</u> internet        <u>38</u>  t.v./VCR

8. How often do YOU use technology for class assignments or projects?

<u>10</u>   daily        <u>28</u>   weekly        <u>36</u>   monthly        <u>6</u>   not at all

9. Which types of technology would YOU like to use for your class work that you currently do not?

<u>15</u> Word processor        <u>35</u>  CD-ROM        <u>16</u>  PC-Viewer
<u>18</u> scanner        <u>25</u>  e-mail        <u>24</u>  computer simulations
<u>34</u> internet        <u>17</u>  t.v./VCR

10. Rank the level of AVAILABILITY of the technology we have in our building.

<u>20</u>   very available        <u>56</u>   somewhat available        <u>2</u>   not available

# 9

# WOODROW WILSON HIGH SCHOOL
## HOW HAS THE BLOCK PERIOD IMPROVED THE QUALITY OF STUDENT LEARNING?

Mike James, Martin Kelly
Joan M. Sikonia, Jerry Thorpe

### SCHOOL PORTRAIT AND INTRODUCTION

Woodrow Wilson High School enrolls 1,800 students, of whom 30 percent are persons of color. The school is in an urban setting in Tacoma, Washington. In September 1994, on the staff-day before students arrived to begin the new school year, the Wilson faculty engaged in an activity called "The Ideal School." In small groups, teachers were to draw what the ideal school would look like, how it would function, and what a typical school day would be. When each group's list of attributes was posted, one element stood out as common to all of the lists. Each group had asked for more quality time to work with students. Teachers felt that the extended time would improve student learning. They wanted the time and the opportunity for students to work on projects, explore, experience, and internalize what they were trying to learn. They wanted to get students in touch with the world of work, and more time in each period would be needed to do this. Teachers wanted to build relationships with the students. They wanted technology and a way to conveniently work with their fellow teachers. They wanted more time to plan and develop new courses and learn new strategies.

At the end of the activity, the Wilson staff decided to use part of the state-provided Student Learning Improvement Grant funds to visit schools in the area that seemed to be enacting the structures and activities articulated in the ideal school exercise. After a series of visits to schools with innovative programs and daily schedules, the staff began to develop a plan to restructure the school day. The four-period day and the three-period day were considered, but changing from a semester to a quarter system was not.

In January 1995, the staff was asked to apply for a federal magnet grant in conjunction with other schools in the district. With the possibility of funds from a grant to implement the "ideal" school, Wilson teachers began to draft a proposal that included a change from the traditional six-period, 55-minute daily schedule to an alternating, three-period day. As a part of the three-period day, teachers would have exactly the same amount of planning time as before, but they would have it every other day in a 110-minute period. The school had to ask the local bargaining unit for a waiver because the three-period day did not offer each high school teacher a minimum of 45-minutes of planning each day.

During this exciting and very challenging time, Wilson also elected its first school-centered decision-making (SCDM) body. The school district had requested that all schools change to a decision-making system that includes certificated and classified staff, parents, and students in the form of an SCDM. After opportunities for input from the staff, the final decision to change from a six-period day to a three-period day was made by consensus of the newly formed SCDM.

The changes for the next school year included the three-period day, a 9th-grade school-within-a-school, total inclusion for the 9th-grade program, and off-campus satellite courses at three community locations. The additional changes were a part of the district magnet grant proposal.

In August, there were six days of paid workshop presentations provided for all staff members. The presenters included experts in the field of cooperative learning, multiple intelligences, the change process, teaching strategies for the inclusion classroom, and techniques for integrative teaching. There were also 3 days when staff members could meet with their own departments or with other departments to develop new lesson plans for the block periods. Approximately 80 percent of the staff participated in these workshops. Many Wilson staff members spent several extra days working to adapt and alter their lesson plans for the block periods.

In September 1995, Wilson High School began to operate on a 110-minute, three-period alternating schedule. Red days were periods 1, 3, and 5; blue days were periods 2, 4, and 6.

## RESEARCH METHODOLOGY

As a part of the decision to try a three-period day, the staff made a commitment to evaluate the effects of the three-period day on student learning; the school climate; student attendance; and student, staff, and parent acceptance of the new schedule. In January, a staff committee was formed to develop the surveys to find out how the new schedule was working. The committee completed its drafts in late January and submitted them to the staff for approval. Revisions were made, and the surveys were sent to the district Research and Development Department to be checked for bias and redundancy.

The parent survey was mailed to each student's home with a postage-paid return envelope included. The staff survey was completed at a staff meeting. The student survey was given in English classes for 9th through 11th grades and in the 12th-grade social studies classes. There was a written script for the SCDM members who administered the student survey to assure a nonbiased presentation of the survey. All surveys were tabulated by Research and Development staff to assure accuracy. (Survey results are included in the appendices.)

The members of the research team also developed an individual free-write question to which we asked teachers to respond: *In what ways has the 110-minute period affected the quality of student learning?* All staff members were requested to answer the question, but 14 teachers representing every department in the school were specifically asked to respond. Of the 14 teachers, 6 replied in writing. The eight others responded verbally.

## FINDINGS AND ANALYSIS

The faculty survey revealed that 70 percent of the staff has used new teaching strategies this year. Sixty-seven percent of the staff like the lengthened class time. Sixty-eight percent have used cooperative learning techniques with students. Sixty-three percent feel that they use the block time effectively. Sixty-five percent have used multiple intelligences techniques in their teaching. Fifty-nine percent feel that there is more student time-on-task. The same percentage feels that classroom achievement has been improved.

Responses to the individual teacher free-write questions suggest that:

♦ Teachers value time with students.

♦ Teachers like the extra time to interact with students.

♦ Teachers feel that they have more freedom to experiment and explore how to present material.

♦ Teachers feel that group work improves the quality of student learning.

♦ Time for students to process what they are learning is valuable.

♦ The block time has helped students have a more positive attitude because they have time to be involved and active in their learning.

♦ Extra time to work with students having difficulty is a positive feature of the three-period day.

Teachers are concerned about the block periods for students with learning difficulties. They feel that for students with a pattern of poor attendance, block periods increase the impact of missed class time.

Teachers' ability to adapt and accept change is a major concern for success of the three-period day.

Positive student comments about the block periods matched those of the teachers in almost all areas. Seventy-five percent of the students like only having three subjects to focus on each day. Students' negative comments indicated that some classes were too long and boring. Some felt that teachers did not use the extra time wisely or ran out of material to present.

Wilson staff also summarized what they felt they had learned from undertaking the faculty survey:

- Asking people for their opinion is very valuable.
- Formally evaluating program changes provides new information.
- Focusing on one issue would improve results.
- More training is essential.
- Teachers need more strategies that involve students in learning.
- Different teaching materials are needed for block-period instruction.
- Continuing to visit schools with successful programs will give staff encouragement and additional skills.
- Teachers have strong feelings about how time is used.
- Don't expect perfection during the first year of a new program.
- Change is difficult.

Teachers' responses to the individual free-response question (*In what ways has the 110-minute period affected the quality of student learning?*) are found in the following paragraphs.

Pepita Sarmiento, Spanish teacher, stated:

Students have improved test scores because we have more time for individualized help, brainstorming ideas during group work, more extended discussion on culture; hence, for students a better knowledge of the world.

Gloria Lee, art teacher, commented:

In the art department, the longer periods make it easier to work on projects and to spend more time with each student. Attendance seems to be better. In craft classes work time is better suited to a longer period so there is less stop/start/clean-up time.

Kay Houg, business education teacher, gave a more detailed answer:

Student learning has been positively affected by the longer periods. In the traditional 55-minute period, a great deal of time was wasted each day completing classroom duties (taking roll, passing out papers, giving directions). By reducing the number of times a student changes classes and the number of times a teacher needs to "start-up" a class, more time can be devoted to instruction. While these few minutes of time may not appear on the surface to be a great advantage to the longer class periods, it has been one of the major changes that has had a positive impact on the time available for instruction to students. In vocational studies where our subjects are often skill-based, the longer periods and classes meeting every other day can be a concern. In introductory keyboarding, beginning students are not prepared to do 2 hours of skill-building drills. However, the 110-minute block of time allows for drill plus time for leadership activities. This spring and summer, the department is meeting to develop a new course syllabus for keyboarding to incorporate some of these activities in the first few weeks of the semester. The greatest advantage to the longer periods is in our advanced labs. Previously, we only had time to introduce a new concept and have the students complete the job and turn it in for evaluation. It was very difficult to critique the students' work as they were completing the assignments. Now we are able to introduce an assignment, assist the students with their questions, and critique their work while the project is being typed. The students do not have to work under rigid time restraints and can proofread their work—they now have sufficient time to do quality checks on their production assignments. The quantity of work has not been increased, but the quality of work has improved.

Mike McKay, social studies and health teacher, stated:

One hundred and ten minutes is too long. I do not cover as much material. I would prefer to see the students daily, regardless of the length of the period. Younger students seem to benefit from daily meetings. My failure rate has been about the same. Students with special needs have more difficulty concentrating and are not finding success with the longer periods. Students who have traditionally had attendance problems are really hurt by the three-period day, because they are missing twice the material by being absent once. It is difficult to schedule guest speakers with the alternating schedule.

Karen Webster, environmental biology teacher, responded:

The extended time period of 110-minutes has enabled the teacher to have more interactive time with students. With the increased length of time spent with each student, more knowledge about learning styles of individual students has opened avenues of creativity in instructional methods that enhance student success. Because more time is spent with the student, a more friendly learning environment is established and students are more successful and positive. There are more opportunities to reinforce not only learning outcomes but also positive learning habits. More students are successful. The teacher can coordinate and organize individual and group learning activities that respond to individual differences and provide more meaningful activities for the students. More variety in laboratory experiences can be accommodated by the block period. It is this writer's view that thinking productively involves discovering and formulating problems, organizing and using information, generating ideas, evaluating and improving ideas, and creating new perspectives....The writer believes the block period encourages teaching that fosters productive responsible thinking for improved student learning.

Dorothy Hudson, family and consumer sciences teacher, stated:

As a family and consumer sciences teacher, I have seen a greater student involvement and achievement on the 110-minute class schedule. We have time to evaluate or summarize more comprehensively. The pace is much less frenetic and stressful. In Foods and other lab classes, there is time to demonstrate and time for students to have the lab while it is still fresh in their minds. Students seem more tuned-in since they know they will be doing the lab the same day. In Child Development, and Marriage and the Family classes, students have been able to hear speakers and have plenty of time to ask the speakers questions. Then, we've been able to debrief after speakers leave while it is still fresh in their minds.

Cecil Stewman, industrial arts teacher, answered the question by mentioning that his students felt more satisfaction because they were able to complete a project and evaluate it with the teacher in fewer class periods. Students seemed to produce higher quality products.

Jerry Collins, language arts teacher, expressed satisfaction with his students' group class work. He felt that group discussions were of higher quality than before, because there was time to have more of them. Students learned to evaluate, assess, and improve their own work. They learned to write and revise so that the final product was better.

Kim Rasmussen, social studies teacher, was concerned that students with learning problems could not handle the long periods. He found that they more easily gave up because they couldn't concentrate. In his opinion, those students susceptible to failure were more likely to fail in the block periods.

Lonnie Slater, social studies teacher, stated that he was originally opposed to the 110-minute period. He teaches the off-campus, satellite course called "Local Perspectives" at the Washington State History Museum. He was impressed by the outstanding, high quality projects that his students were producing. He commented that this course would not be possible under the old 55-minute six-period day.

Jerry Thorpe, a Wilson social studies teacher, still had serious concerns about improved learning for students who were less capable and who had a short attention span, but he was positive about the satellite campus course he teaches at Tacoma's World Trade Center. This class would not have been possible with shorter periods, and he saw the benefit students had gained by being exposed to firsthand knowledge about the functions of the Port of Tacoma.

Ken Marks, mathematics teacher, stated that the block period allows him more time to work with individual students and to be sure they understand and can apply the new concepts he was introducing. He said that the block period allows for use of technology to aid students in learning, practicing, and applying new math skills.

Judy Montague, family and consumer sciences teacher, stated that she felt students seemed more involved, more active, more concerned about their learning. She liked having the time to get to know the students, finding out about their learning styles, and planning group activities for students to gain self-confidence and better communication skills. Students had time to work in groups, do individual research, and plan and practice an oral presentation. There was time also for students to talk about and evaluate the presentations.

Rosalyn Fannin, language arts teacher, was concerned about students with poor basic skills. She felt that better students were more successful with the block periods, but that less capable students had more difficulty concentrating.

## OUTCOMES AND CONCLUSION

One significant way in which the curriculum at Wilson changed as a result of the block periods is the satellite campus courses. Three new courses were developed to promote students' awareness of career opportunities, to provide an integrated teaching environment, and to increase students' marketable skills by providing on-site learning in the community. In these courses students have the time to leave campus to attend sessions provided by professionals in the community. Marine Biology is taught at Tacoma's Point Defiance Zoo and Aquarium. The education director of the zoo and aquarium provides leadership for the class sessions together with the school biology teacher Pat Bishop. The students have frequent opportunities to observe and be trained as helpers to the professional aquarists in their work. They see and learn from marine biologists as they use their science skills and knowledge in the workplace. A portion of the class time is dedicated to studying the movement of tides, waves, and currents. Because the zoo and aquarium is located on Puget Sound, the students can study firsthand the physical and chemical properties of ocean waters. Water quality measurements are taken. Students see the connection of these measurements to the health and safety of the aquarium sea life. Students will be provided training and spend volunteer time as docents for the zoo and aquarium exhibits. This activity will be an integral part of the class requirements. Because of the success of the program, additional sections of this class will be provided.

Students who are enrolled in another of Wilson's satellite courses, U.S. History Through Local Perspectives, have also benefited from the block periods. They attend class at Tacoma's Washington State History Museum, taught by Lonnie Slatter, and have the opportunity to study multiple aspects of history—interpretation and preservation, as well as content. They are actively involved in using the displays and research materials at the museum to view U.S. history as applied to people, places, and events in local Washington State history. Students use authentic documents to make learning history interactive and relevant. There is also an opportunity for students to become trained as museum interpreters. Students develop museum displays as a part of their research and project-oriented learning experience.

Wilson's third satellite course is International and Domestic Economics. It is located at Tacoma's World Trade Center for the Port of Tacoma and is taught by Jerry Thorpe, a Wilson faculty member who is also a Tacoma Port Commissioner. Students are allowed to see firsthand what is involved in the development and management of local businesses that engage in international and domestic trade through the Port of Tacoma. Students view and are involved in discussions with leaders from businesses. They learn about advertising, finance, port operations, legal issues, use of technology, and the environmental concerns of the Port of Tacoma.

The Wilson staff hopes to expand the satellite campus courses to include other community sites, which might include the local court system for an Advanced Legal Occupations course or students learning and working with local artists, musicians, and writers in their businesses and studios for an Applied Arts course.

Wilson's block-period schedule encouraged and allowed teachers to expand the boundaries of the learning environment for students away from the traditional school building out into the community. The school has been able to forge new connections for students and teachers with the community and the world of work. Students are able to see the knowledge that they are trying to learn as it functions in the real world. Teachers and students are being revitalized by seeing academic skills and knowledge applied to solving problems in a work environment. Teachers are learning from and working with their professional counterparts in the community.

After the Wilson staff considered the results of the faculty survey in a staff meeting, discussed teachers' major concerns, and reviewed the question of the quality of student learning, the Wilson SCDM proposed to continue with the three-period day. The staff requested continued training to provide them with more teaching strategies. They asked for materials that are designed to provide active skill building with students. Teachers requested more school-to-work and applied learning materials and information. They asked for help to improve learning for students at-risk. The staff would like to continue to visit schools with innovative and successful programs in block periods.

Wilson teachers have spent a great deal of extra effort making several major changes in the way they teach and in what they teach. They have attempted to adapt, adjust, and learn new skills. They risked making a change in order to improve student learning. They were willing to ask parents and students what they think of their teaching. Staff is continuing to rethink how students learn and teachers teach. Teachers are still in the process of identifying concerns and recognizing strengths. They are rethinking the opportunities for learning that are provided by teaching in block periods. They have decided to focus on the quality of student learning and improved instruction in block periods for next year.

(Mr. James teaches art. Mr. Kelly teaches social studies. Ms. Sikonia teaches foreign languages and is the curriculum resource teacher. Mr. Thorpe teaches social studies.)

## CRITICAL COMMENTS

Leslie Nuttman and Toni Smith, who teach at North Mason High School in Belfair, Washington, wrote most of the following comments. David Marshak added several elements to this commentary.

## RESEARCH ANALYSIS

Wilson's research question (*In what ways has the 110-minute period affected the quality of student learning?*) is relevant in light of the number of high schools that have changed or are considering changing to some type of block- or extended-period day. It is interesting to the same groups of people because there is not a lot of data available on this topic at this time. As educators, it is a question to which we would very much like to have pragmatic answers.

Unfortunately, the "quality of student learning" is a very difficult concept to define or measure accurately. This research project never clearly defines what components of this concept it wants to measure. The project could have been improved by clarifying the question so that it would be clear what factors were to be studied.

The research process based itself on surveys given to teachers, students, and parents. Teacher surveys were given out at a faculty meeting, and there were 92 respondents. Student surveys were given to all grades during class time with a return rate of 1,132 out of 1,797. Parent surveys were mailed to all parents, with a return of 295. All teachers were asked to provide free-write essays expressing their beliefs and feelings about the block day. Fourteen teachers were specifically asked to respond in order to represent all departments. Six responded in writing; eight responded verbally. It is unknown if any other staff responded, as there are only 14 responses in the report.

All the data presented catalogue perceptions on questions ranging from "Staff members are flexible and have adapted to new situations" to "Attendance has improved in my classes" to "I feel school is less stressful because of the lengthened periods." A concern is the category "Not applicable" (NA) as a response choice to questions such as "I have used a variety of assessment methods to evaluate my students." Twenty-three percent of staff respondents chose NA. How could this not be applicable to a teaching respondent? A teacher either has or has not "used a variety of assessment methods." The staff questionnaire included teachers, administrators, and classified staff respondents, which might explain the high number of NA responses. The research could have been clarified by separating classroom teachers from other high school staff so that responses about teaching procedures and perceptions would not be skewed by a large number of NA answers from those who are not directly involved in classroom instruction. It is not clear why classified staff were asked questions about teaching strategies. (It might have been valuable to Wilson High School to survey its classified staff regarding the impact of block-period days on their jobs and responsibilities, though this would not have been directly relevant to this research question.)

Another question regarding the research process relates to Wilson's full restructuring efforts and their overall impact on the "quality of student learning." The block-period day was instituted along with proposed satellite courses, a proposed school-within-a-school, curriculum changes, and full inclusion for the 9th-grade program. It would be impossible to factor out the block-period day and to say which results came only from it.

In our experience, a one-sixth return from parent questionnaires is quite high and Wilson is to be commended. A concern is, how much do parents really know about "My child's teachers offer more in-depth material with the three-period day?" Are they truly knowledgeable about curriculum or are they reflecting their child's attitude? Other parent questions were within the realm of parent knowledge.

At some point Wilson might find it helpful to define the "quality of student learning" more specifically to include hard data from sources such as standardized test scores or achievement of identified essential learnings.

A final reminder about the research process would be not to draw too many hard and fast conclusions based on 1 year of a changed schedule. North Mason's answers after 1 year looked much different than they would look today after 4 years on a block-period schedule.

The Wilson report states that the "staff made a commitment to evaluate the effect of the three-period day on student learning, the school climate, student attendance, and parent acceptance of the new schedule." We feel the research and findings do an excellent job of assessing many aspects of the schedule change, *except* for student learning. It still seems necessary to be very purposeful in defining what precisely measures *student learning* and *quality.*

In several places, generalizations were made about the responses to the surveys and the percentages of approval and disapproval. For instance, the researchers conclude that "group work improves the quality of student learning," but the support for that statement is again the survey results that report staff *perceptions* of changes and improvements since instituting the block period schedule. Many data were reported, but we find ourselves still unsure of what this action research team has concluded about the quality of student learning as it relates to the new schedule.

Wilson intends to continue the block period day in 1996–1997. Staff have requested additional training, materials, and help with improving learning for students at risk. They would also like to continue to visit schools with successful block-day programs. It is not clear from the report whether or not these resources will be provided, but they would address many of the concerns of staff members. Continuation of the 110-minute periods will allow Wilson to continue their satellite classes, which appear to be quite successful. Staff members have decided to focus on the quality of student learning and improved instruction in block periods for the 1996–97 school year. If they seriously want to measure these elements, they need to define these terms carefully at the outset and decide what kinds of factors make up quality student learning and improved instruction.

## FINAL THOUGHTS

First, the data from the teacher survey generally support the hypothesis that many teachers at Wilson High School have begun to abandon the conventional model of high school in favor of some new set of structural values and guidelines.

However, the data are limited in that, as noted earlier, they present teachers' perceptions about these issues at a single point in the first year of their implementation of a block-period schedule.

Second, the impact of block periods and the ways in which the structure is affecting the teaching practice of Wilson's teachers are more graphically illustrated in the teacher comments, such as the following:

> In the art department, the longer periods make it easier to work on projects and to spend more time with each student.

> Now we are able to introduce an assignment, assist the students with their questions, and critique their work while the project is being typed. The students do not have to work under rigid time restraints and can proofread their work. They now have sufficient time to do quality checks on their production assignments. The quantity of work has not been increased, but the quality of work has improved.

> Because more time is spent with the student, a more friendly learning environment is established and students are more successful and positive. There are more opportunities to reinforce not only learning outcomes but also positive learning habits.

> The teacher can coordinate and organize individual and group learning activities that respond to individual differences and provide more meaningful activities for the students.

> I have seen a greater student involvement and achievement on the 110-minute class schedule. We have time to evaluate or summarize more comprehensively. The pace is much less frenetic and stressful.

> In Foods and other lab classes, there is time to demonstrate and time for students to have the lab while it is still fresh in their minds. Students seem more tuned-

in since they know they will be doing the lab the same day.

Group discussions were of higher quality than before, because there was time to have more of them. Students learned to evaluate, assess, and improve their own work. They learned to write and revise so that the final product was better.

Students seemed more involved, more active, more concerned about their learning....Students had time to work in groups, do individual research, plan and practice an oral presentation. There was also time for students to talk about and evaluate the presentations.

Third, several teachers raise the concern that "weaker students" are not well served by block periods. Mr. McKay, for example, explains, "Students with special needs have more difficulty concentrating and are not finding success with the longer periods. Students who have traditionally had attendance problems are really hurt by the three-period day, because they are missing twice the material by being absent once." Ms. Fannin feels that "less capable students had more difficulty concentrating." This concern definitely requires further evaluation and ongoing monitoring. It raises many questions that cannot be answered with the data available. For example: Is the problem described in relation to student concentration a factor within the structure of the block itself or in the teaching methods applied? Is the attendance problem described a given or can the nature of block classes alter student behavior in relation to attendance?

Finally, the three satellite courses are examples of the kinds of connected learning, to use the Tahoma team's category and concept, that could not have happened without block periods. From their descriptions, these courses all seem to be significant steps out of "the box" of the conventional model of high school.

## APPENDIX 9.1. SURVEY RESULTS

### Staff Highlights

Seventy-nine percent (79%) of staff feel adequately prepared to face the challenges of restructuring and 74% feel they are kept informed of developments that affect the restructuring efforts.

Staff are almost evenly split on whether the channels of communication between members, and between staff and the administration, are open and functioning adequately. Seventy-six percent (76%), however, agree the administrative staff have been supportive of the restructuring efforts.

Two-thirds (67%) of the staff like or really like the three-period day.

Seventy percent (70%) indicate they have used new teaching strategies this year. Half of the staff either agree or strongly agree that with the three-period day students have better comprehension of the material presented.

The staff is also split on the impact the restructuring efforts have had on students:

     50% indicate attendance has improved
     43% indicate student performance has improved
     51% indicate student conduct has improved

Staff comments to the open-ended items indicate that the most frequently cited positive feature of Wilson's restructuring efforts is the increased time for one-on-one assistance to students. The most cited negative feature is the resistance to change among some Wilson staff.

### Parents' Highlights

Parents' survey responses are generally favorable. Sixty-nine percent (69%) feel their child's classroom achievement has been helped by the extended periods and 62% feel more in-depth material is now being offered.

Twenty-nine percent (29%) of the respondents feel the 9th grade school-within-a-school program has been beneficial, while 10% feel it has not been beneficial. Most parents (62%) indicated "not applicable" or they did not respond, presumably because they did not have a ninth grader.

The satellite programs also received favorable responses from the parents who marked a response to this item. Nearly half (49%) of the respondents agreed that these programs offer additional learning and career opportunities; 5% disagreed. The remaining 45% did not offer an opinion.

Two items received more mixed results. First, 45% of respondents indicated their child feels safer this year than last year, but 28% indicated this is not true for their child, and 27% of the parents did not indicate a response (perhaps because their child did not attend Wilson last year). Second, 37% of the parents feel the three-period day has improved their child's attendance, but 29% feel it has not.

The parents' responses were split between favorable and unfavorable comments. Twenty-four parents specified that they like the three-period day, and 20 parents stated they were generally pleased. However, 23 parents indicated general dissatisfaction with the changes, 17 indicated the three-period day is not a good use of class time, and 16 commented the classes are too long.

## Students' Highlights

A large majority (79%) of students like only having three subjects to focus on each day.

Sixty-three (63%) indicate they are more productive with this schedule, and 58% feel they are more organized.

Fifty-eight (58%) of the students agreed that their teachers offer more in-depth material, but only a slight majority (51%) feel their teachers are more effective with the lengthened periods.

Fifty-three (53%) feel they get more individual attention from their teachers.

Student comments to the open-ended items indicate that the most frequently cited positive feature of Wilson's three-period day is the increased time (2 or more nights) to do homework (this was cited by 37% of the students). Also frequently cited (by 34%) was the increased amount of time for completing work in class, thus reducing the amount of homework.

The most cited negative feature is that the classes are boring (cited by 46% of the students). Twenty-five percent (25%) of the students indicated the classes are too long, and 21% of the students indicated that teachers don't use the extra time wisely and/or run out of material midway through the period.

* Survey assistance provided by the Tacoma Public Schools, Department of Planning, Research and Evaluation (Sharon Langren, Maria Womack, Robin Munson)

## APPENDIX 9.2. STAFF QUESTIONNAIRE

WILSON HIGH SCHOOL
STAFF QUESTIONNAIRE
N=92

Your primary role at Wilson:

85% - (1) teacher/other certificated
11% - (2) paraprofessional/other classified
4% - (3) administrator

Number of years at Wilson:

9% - (1) One year or less
23% - (2) Two to four years
30% - (3) Five to nine years
38% - (4) Ten or more years

List all departments in which you have taught:

13% - Physical Education
25% - English/Library
2% - Family & Consumer
Science
17% - Mathematics
9% - Business

1% - Industrial Arts
16% - Social Studies
7% - Special Education
8% - Foreign Language
2% - Music

3% - Art
13% - Science
8% - Classified
20% - Other

Please use the following scale to respond to each item below:

| 1 | 2 | 3 | 4 | NA |

strongly agree.........agree............disagree.......strongly disagree.......not applicable

| | 1 | 2 | 3 | 4 | NA |
|---|---|---|---|---|---|
| TRAINING<br>I received adequate training and information in August 1995 to prepare for the changes before they went into effect. | 28% | 38% | 14% | 13% | 7% |
| I feel adequately prepared to face challenges related to restructuring. | 33% | 46% | 12% | 9% | 1% |
| COMMUNICATION<br>I am kept informed of developments that affect our restructuring efforts. | 27% | 47% | 13% | 12% | 1% |
| The channels of communication between staff members are open and functioning adequately. | 10% | 35% | 35% | 14% | 7% |
| The channels of communication between staff members and administration are open and functioning adequately. | 12% | 35% | 29% | 18% | 5% |
| JOB RESPONSIBILITIES<br>I teach effectively with a planning period every other day. | 27% | 22% | 11% | 18% | 22% |
| I have used new teaching strategies this year. | 37% | 33% | 7% | 4% | 20% |

| | | | | | |
|---|---|---|---|---|---|
| INTERPERSONAL RELATIONS<br>Staff members are flexible and have adapted to new situations. | 9% | 46% | 30% | 10% | 5% |
| Staff members deal effectively with new problems and challenges as they arise. | 9% | 51% | 26% | 8% | 7% |
| Problems related to restructuring are in the process of being resolved. | 16% | 38% | 23% | 13% | 10% |
| SUPPORT<br>The building administrative staff have been supportive of our restructuring efforts. | 25% | 51% | 15% | 9% | |
| Building staff have been supportive of our restructuring efforts. | 7% | 48% | 34% | 11% | 1% |
| GENERAL FEELINGS<br>I like the lengthened class time of the three-period day. | 47% | 20% | 13% | 17% | 3% |
| I would prefer the three-period day if it included planning time every day. | 38% | 22% | 10% | 11% | 20% |
| CURRICULUM<br>With the three-period day I have used cooperative learning techniques with my students. | 33% | 35% | 7% | 4% | 22% |
| I have used a variety of assessment methods to evaluate my students. | 25% | 42% | 5% | 4% | 23% |
| I have been able to effectively use the extended class time. | 34% | 29% | 14% | 6% | 16% |
| I have incorporated multiple intelligences techniques into my teaching style. | 22% | 43% | 8% | 3% | 24% |
| With the three-period day students have better comprehension of the material presented. | 21% | 29% | 20% | 17% | 13% |
| With the three-period day there is more student time-on-task. | 26% | 32% | 17% | 15% | 10% |
| SCHOOL ATMOSPHERE<br>Attendance has improved in my classes. | 23% | 27% | 20% | 12% | 18% |
| Tardiness has decreased this year. | 16% | 25% | 28% | 14% | 16% |
| Student performance has improved in my classes. | 17% | 26% | 24% | 12% | 21% |
| Student conduct has improved this year. | 21% | 30% | 21% | | 12% |
| The ten-minute break is an appropriate expenditure of time. | 32% | 35% | 16% | 6% | 11% |
| The extended period has helped classroom achievement. | 24% | 25% | 21% | 13% | 17% |
| The school environment is a safer place. | 23% | 33% | 15% | 10% | 20.% |

## APPENDIX 9.3. STAFF SURVEY COMMENTS

WILSON STAFF SURVEY COMMENTS
N=92

| The *best* features of restructuring at Wilson are: | Count | Percent | The *worst* features of restructuring at Wilson are: | Count | Percent |
|---|---|---|---|---|---|
| more time (one on one) with students | 32 | 35% | resistance to change among colleagues | 24 | 26% |
| projects are easier to plan | 15 | 16% | no time for planning | 15 | 16% |
| fewer behavior problems | 9 | 10% | students need daily contact with teachers | 13 | 14% |
| class planning easier | 9 | 10% | students are bored | 12 | 13% |
| hectic pace reduced | 8 | 9% | no communication with staff about restructuring | 6 | 7% |
| less hall movement | 8 | 9% | poor attendance (students get behind if absent) | 5 | 5% |
| everything | 6 | 7% | staff never voted to adopt the 3 period day | 5 | 5% |
| attendance is better | 5 | 5% | afternoon break is needed | 3 | 3% |
| 9th grade program successful | 5 | 5% | inclusion without support | 3 | 3% |
| grades are better | 4 | 4% | grades have not improved | 2 | 2% |
|  |  |  | long time between classes if holiday, snow make-up, etc. | 2 | 2% |

## APPENDIX 9.4. PARENT SURVEY

WILSON HIGH SCHOOL PARENT SURVEY
N=295

| To what extent do you agree with the following statements? | Strongly Agree | Agree | Disagree | Strongly Disagree | NA | No Response |
|---|---|---|---|---|---|---|
| 1. The extended period has helped my son or daughter's classroom achievement. | 28% | 41% | 15% | 12% | 3% | 1% |
| 2. My son or daughter feels safer this year than last year. | 9% | 36% | 20% | 8% | 23% | 4% |
| 3. My child's teachers offer more in-depth material with the three-period day. | 18% | 44% | 18% | 14% | 4% | 2% |
| 4. The satellite programs offer additional learning and career opportunities. | 20% | 29% | 2% | 3% | 44% | 1% |
| 5. The ninth grade school-within-a-school has benefitted my son or daughter. | 10% | 19% | 4% | 6% | 61% | 1% |
| 6. My child's attendance has improved with the three-period day. | 12% | 25% | 20% | 9% | 31% | 2% |

## APPENDIX 9.5. PARENT COMMENTS

WILSON **PARENT** SURVEY COMMENTS
N=295

| Comments: | Count | Percent |
|---|---|---|
| like extended periods | 24 | 8% |
| generally dislike | 23 | 8% |
| generally pleased | 20 | 7% |
| not good use of class time | 17 | 6% |
| classes are too long | 16 | 5% |
| long classes are too boring | 11 | 4% |
| don't change start time | 8 | 3% |
| change school hours | 7 | 2% |
| need breaks/need more breaks | 6 | 2% |
| not enough in-depth instruction | 4 | 1% |
| can accomplish more in class | 2 | 1% |
| less homework | 2 | 1% |
| don't like the 9th grade wing | 2 | 1% |
| walk around schedule needs improvement | 2 | 1% |
| students are failing more | 1 | 0% |
| dangerous | 1 | 0% |
| not many satellite "programs" offered | 1 | 0% |

# APPENDIX 9.6. STUDENT SURVEY

### WILSON HIGH SCHOOL
### STUDENT SURVEY
### N=1132

Please use the following scale to respond to each item below:

| 1 | 2 | 3 | 4 | NA |
|---|---|---|---|----|
| strongly agree | agree | disagree | strongly disagree | not applicable |

| | 1 | 2 | 3 | 4 | NA | No Response |
|---|---|---|---|---|---|---|
| I feel safer at Wilson High School this year. | 8.7% | 34.7% | 15.9% | 6.6% | 33.4% | 0.8% |
| I am more productive with the new schedule. | 19.4% | 44.5% | 19.2% | 9.5% | 6.1% | 0.9% |
| I like having only three subjects to focus on each day. | 44.9% | 34.2% | 9.0% | 9.1% | 2.2% | 0.6% |
| I get more individual attention from my teachers with the lengthened periods. | 16.6% | 36.2% | 29.0% | 12.4% | 5.3% | 0.6% |
| I feel school is less stressful because of the lengthened periods. | 20.3% | 31.6% | 26.0% | 16.2% | 5.2% | 0.7% |
| I have more homework with the lengthened periods. | 16.8% | 26.3% | 35.9% | 15.6% | 4.6% | 0.9% |
| I am more organized with the lengthened periods. | 17.4% | 40.6% | 24.3% | 9.8% | 7.0% | 0.9% |
| The lengthened periods have helped me develop more friendly relationships with other students. | 15.9% | 40.4% | 23.6% | 8.0% | 11.2% | 0.9% |
| I feel my teachers are more effective with the lengthened periods. | 12.1% | 39.1% | 27.4% | 12.3% | 8.3% | 0.8% |
| My grades are generally better than they were last year. | 18.2% | 30.6% | 25.9% | 13.2% | 11.3% | 0.8% |
| I feel my teachers offer more in-depth materials with the three-period day. | 14.3% | 43.8% | 25.5% | 8.3% | 7.4% | 0.8% |
| My attendance has improved with the three-period day. | 16.3% | 28.2% | 26.3% | 12.8% | 15.6% | 0.7% |

| | 9th | 10th | 11th | 12th | | No Response |
|---|---|---|---|---|---|---|
| I am in grade: | 30.8% | 27.0% | 21.6% | 19.2% | ------- | 1.4% |

| | 4.0-3.5 | 3.4-2.5 | 2.4-1.5 | 1.4 or below | not sure | No Response |
|---|---|---|---|---|---|---|
| My grade point average is within the range of: | 30.6% | 46.4% | 12.6% | 1.8% | 7.1% | 1.6% |

| | 0-2 days missed | 3-5 days missed | 6 or more days missed | | | No Response |
|---|---|---|---|---|---|---|
| My attendance is within the range of: | 42.8% | 38.9% | 13.7% | | | 4.6% |

## APPENDIX 9.7. STUDENT COMMENTS

WILSON STUDENT SURVEY COMMENTS
N=250 (randomly selected from 1132 completed)

| The *best* things about having the school day divided into three periods are: | Count | Percent | The *worst* things about having the school day divided into three periods are: | Count | Percent |
|---|---|---|---|---|---|
| 2 or more nights for homework | 93 | 37% | classes are boring | 116 | 46% |
| more time to do work in class so less homework | 86 | 34% | periods are too long | 62 | 25% |
| school is more relaxed; only 3 classes to worry about | 41 | 16% | teachers don't use time wisely/run out of material | 52 | 21% |
| more time in the good classes | 38 | 15% | too much homework | 40 | 16% |
| more time for help | 37 | 15% | hurts to sit that long | 38 | 15% |
| time to get to know classmates and teachers | 24 | 10% | missing one day is actually like missing two | 23 | 9% |
| projects/labs are easier | 19 | 8% | need breaks | 22 | 9% |
| variety is nice; don't have to see teachers everyday | 15 | 6% | easy to forget or postpone homework | 19 | 8% |
| longer lunch | 14 | 6% | fall asleep | 18 | 7% |
| longer passing time | 14 | 6% | confusing schedule | 16 | 6% |
| fewer books to carry | 11 | 4% | general dislike | 16 | 6% |
| can focus on each subject | 6 | 2% | forget content from day to day | 13 | 5% |
| more time to sleep in class | 6 | 2% | have to spend time with teacher/friend you don't like | 12 | 5% |
| better teaching | 5 | 2% | encourages skipping | 9 | 4% |
| more in-depth instruction | 4 | 2% | some classes need every day for continuity | 6 | 4% |
| encourages attendance | 3 | 1% | don't see friends everyday | 6 | 4% |
| only miss 3 subjects when absent | 1 | 0% | too much material covered | 5 | 2% |
| less interruption in starting/stopping | 1 | 0% | nothing bad about it | 3 | 1% |
| more time for finishing tests | 1 | 0% | | | |
| nothing good about it | 1 | 0% | | | |